The Critical Decade

The Critical Decade

An Economic Policy for America and the Free World

by Congressman Henry S. Reuss

McGraw-Hill Book Company

NEW YORK   TORONTO   LONDON

THE CRITICAL DECADE

I am grateful to the following publishers and authors for permission to quote from the works named below:

The United States and the Western Community by Haviland Field, reprinted by permission of the Corporation of Haverford College, 1957.

The London Financial Times, July, 1963, reprinted by permission of Charles Croot.

The *Journal of Business*, January, 1963, "Business Spending and Government Fiscal Policy," by Walter D. Fackler, reprinted by permission of The University of Chicago Press. Copyright © 1963 by The University of Chicago.

The Economist, October 19, 1957, reprinted by permission of The Economist Newspaper Ltd.

The Deadlock of Democracy by James MacGregor Burns, reprinted by permission of Prentice-Hall, Inc., 1963.

The Edge of the Sword by Charles De Gaulle, reprinted by permission of Criterion Books, Inc., 1932.

Congressional Government by Woodrow Wilson, reprinted by permission of the Houghton Mifflin Company, 1885.

MEMOIRS, Vol. III, *Salvation,* by Charles De Gaulle, reprinted by permission of Simon & Schuster, 1960.

Restless Nations: A Study of World Tensions and Development, Council on World Tensions, reprinted by permission of Dodd, Mead & Company, 1962.

The Forge of Democracy by Neil MacNeil, reprinted by permission of the David McKay Company, 1963.

"Multilateral versus Bilateral Aid: An Old Controversy Revisited" by Robert E. Asher, reprinted from *International Organization*, Autumn, 1962.

The Customs Union Issue by Jacob Viner, reprinted by permission of the Carnegie Endowment for International Peace, 1950.

The Rescue of the Dollar by Wilson E. Schmidt, reprinted by permission of the American Enterprise Institute, 1963.

Foreign Affairs, October, 1962, "Cooperation is not Enough," by Sir Oliver Franks, reprinted by permission of the Council on Foreign Relations, Inc.

Georgetown Law Review, Spring, 1963, "The Trade Expansion Act of 1962," by Stanley Metzger, reprinted by permission of the Georgetown Law Journal Association.

Law and Politics by Felix Frankfurter, reprinted by permission of Harcourt Brace & World, 1939.

UK, Common Wealth and Common Market, by James D. Meade, reprinted by permission of the Institute of Economic Affairs, 1962.

The United States and the Unity of Europe, by Max Beloff, reprinted by permission of The Brookings Institution, 1963.

The European Common Market by Isaiah Frank, reprinted by permission of Frederick A. Praeger, Inc., 1961.

International Payments and Exchange Rates, reprinted by permission of the Chamber of Commerce of the United States of America, 1963.

Business Week, January 26, 1963, "The Right Remedy, but Late and Little," reprinted by permission of McGraw-Hill Publishing Company.

The New Yorker of January 19, 1963, "The Invisible Poor," by Dwight Macdonald, reprinted by permission of original publication, *The New Yorker*.

New York Times Magazine, April 7, 1963, article by Hubert H. Humphrey, reprinted 1963 by The New York Times Company. Reprinted by permission

To Chris, Mike, Jackie, and Anne

Preface

I found 1963 an appropriate year in which to write this book. The occasion was the forceful convergence of domestic and international events which called into doubt many of the policies we have been pursuing since World War II. What I have to say is stated with some specificity, in order that public opinion may have the opportunity to agree or disagree. To some, it may seem that I am excessively preoccupied with economics. If this is so, it is not because I believe that man lives by bread alone. It is rather because I believe that the economic strength of the United States and the free world is fundamental to the success of all our objectives at home and abroad. I thought it wise to limit myself to economic problems, since it is these to which I have devoted most of my attention since I came to Congress.

Felix Frankfurter's delineation of our economic problems, domestic and foreign, back in 1933 is applicable thirty years later:

The way out lies in bold and laborious grappling with the basic forces of our economic situation. But we have been told and are still told, that the path of wisdom cannot be faced and that the hard road of action that we ought to take cannot be taken because public opinion will not support it. I have not believed it in the past and I believe it still less today. The one generalization that can fairly be made about public opinion is that the public responds to truth-telling and courage in high places. Moreover, the function of political leadership is to lead, and not to allow action to be paralyzed because public opinion is confused and distracted. I venture the belief that never have our people been more ripe or more ready to follow determined direction based upon a brave and lucid analysis of our economic forces. I venture to believe that that applies to the international aspects of our national problem no less than to our immediate domestic issues.

This book was all but complete before President John F. Kennedy was slain by an assassin's bullet on November 22, 1963. In the aftermath of that bitter day, I would wish only to reinforce the recommendations for action that are made in this book. Where some of President Kennedy's policies need development or adaptation, this is to recognize changed circumstances as he himself would have done had he lived. Just as fledgling aviators are sent immediately into the air after one of them crashes, so we, after this tragedy, can healthfully substitute morbid grief for efforts beyond the ordinary in order to meet the challenges of our time.

Grateful acknowledgment must go to Sidney Hyman for suggesting this book; to Mrs. Edna Gass and V. Everard Munsey for their thought and help every step of the way; to James W. Knowles, William H. Moore, and Gerald Pollack of the staff of the Congressional Joint Economic Committee; to George Galloway, Hermann Ficker, and Asher Aschenstein of the Legislative Reference Service of the Library of Congress; to Mrs. Sara Robinson, Miss Morvie Colby, and Mrs. Irene Cripps for their labors on the script; and to my wife, Margaret.

Henry S. Reuss
Washington, D.C.

Contents

Foreword

In economic matters, there is no advantage and, on the whole, some peril in being first with a rational point of view. Quite a few people anticipated the Keynesian position on budgets and fiscal policy. They were dismissed as crackpots, and Keynes' own escape may have been narrow. For a long time, while I was working on *The Affluent Society,* and without suggesting too pretentious a parallel, I wondered if my case for the diminishing urgency of private production and a better balance between public services and private goods would not be dismissed as eccentric. I have always felt that the first Russian Sputnik, with its warning that we couldn't rely on General Motors for everything, was what saved me.

Congressman Reuss is a lawyer who is also a first-rate economist. I like to think that he owes something to an early association with the Office of Price Administration—where he was Assistant General Counsel and economists were available in abundance. A more important reason, I reluctantly suspect, is a prodigious appetite for ideas and information and an insistent tendency to think things out for himself. This book is evidence on both counts. In particular, it contains the fresh and informed views of a man who does his own homework and his own thinking.

His chapter on international trade policy is the best example of his dangerous talent for being ahead of his time. There is no subject on which liberals are more completely—and dangerously—committed to their clichés and to the past. This led them to accept, with equanimity and in the name of European unity, sharp tariff increases against our products. For that, from our point of view, is the effect of the formation of the

Common Market, with the averaging of external tariffs (including the averaging up of the vital ones) and the elimination of internal tariffs. Now, in the new round of bargaining, the Common Market countries are in the happy position of being able to offer concessions on numerous products, notably machinery and industrial products, where the present production is more than adequate or price has little effect on sales. Our concessions will be on consumers' goods, where the effect on sales will be immediate and where the effect on the dollar outflow will be seriously adverse. But none of this is new. Congressman Reuss pointed to these dangers several years ago. While more will agree with him now, he cannot hope to be forgiven for being right too soon.

His insight extends to numerous other issues. It is customary when an economist writes an introduction to the book of even his best friend to disdain full agreement. "This is a challenging book, even though I cannot accept quite all of it." In one or two places, I sense that Congressman Reuss is gently disagreeing with some of my views. Here I can hardly avoid entering a reservation. But I do so reluctantly because the book is not only challenging but comes to the right conclusion.

John Kenneth Galbraith

CHAPTER ONE

The Watershed of 1963

> We live in an age of uncertainty. So many rules have been broken, prophecies proved false, and doctrines shown to be baseless; so many trials, losses and disappointments have been inflicted upon us, so many shocks and surprises, that the established order has been strained and shaken.
>
> Charles de Gaulle (1932), *The Edge of the Sword*

Faced by a great issue of state, the rulers of ancient Macedonia first considered the case when drunk, then reconsidered it when sober. If the decision reached was the same either way, they acted on it, being convinced that it combined boldness and prudence.

I do not advocate replacing our own constitutional procedures with the Macedonian method. Yet its boldness and prudence could be used on the great questions our own times put to us.

What are we doing about the task now facing us on the common frontier where domestic and foreign policy meet—the task of building the economic and political foundations for a free world community? Are we attacking it with boldness and prudence—or reacting to it with the aimless frenzy of the cat on the hot tin roof? By what we do through foresight and planning, are we producing the events we want to have happen on that common frontier—or are we merely awaiting the onset of events shaped by others before we decide what to do?

These questions take their force from the fact that until recent months the policies we framed in the immediate aftermath of World War II seemed a reliable plan of action to follow. That certainty is now shaken. Wherever we look, we see how events on the move—some the children of our own postwar success—have outstripped the reach of our plans. History itself, which seemed until recently to decree that our tomorrows would be precisely like our todays, has become fluid again.

This in turn means that we must become once again, not a chosen people, but a *choosing* people who voluntarily impose on themselves the burden—and who invite the glory—of seeking to advance mankind's best hopes. It means that under wholly new circumstances we must bring to bear even greater social invention and resolution than when America first reconciled itself to two realities: that it was a world power, and that the price of power entailed global responsibilities.

That act of reconciliation was not easy. We were, to be sure, never really isolated from the world around us. At the very outset of our life as an independent nation, we were not only deeply involved in the conflicts of the great nations of Europe, but we turned those conflicts to our own advantage. Yet at the close of the 18th century and throughout the 19th, we felt ourselves at liberty either to do without allies or to limit any alliance to the length of a war. Either way, the aim was to pick our friends and enemies one at a time, by the measure of the land they held or could help us get in our expansionist march from the Atlantic to the Pacific.

Even when the center of American action moved from a continental to an oceanic diplomacy toward the close of the 19th century, our external relations were mostly with people much like ourselves. Our greatest fear of other powers was that they might reduce our access to the physical assets we wanted. We could be reasonably sure that, whatever the issue, our internal social order would remain relatively unchanged.

For this reason, we could choose to concentrate now on

foreign affairs, now on domestic. If we erred in one place, the result tended to be self-sealing. Fate, having its own purposes in mind, gave us two oceans, a virgin continent, and a margin of years when we could be free of disruptive outside inter- ference. By trial and error, therefore, we could store up a treasure house of moods, ideas, moral energy, and sheer physi- cal might as we refined and enlarged the meaning of freedom in all its dimensions—political, economic, social, and intel- lectual. It was as though we were allowed all this so that we could better serve the Western tradition at the moment when it was most seriously menaced.

Plunged into World War II by the world we had previously dealt with at a distance, we won decisive battlefield victories. But the policies for the postwar world formulated during the war scarcely survived the victory parades of our returning armies. Our wartime hopes for a peaceful future were founded on the vision of an undivided world, governed by an effective international organization. It was too simple a vision, and it proved one of the first of the postwar casualties.

We failed to give due weight to the ancient truth that nature abhors a vacuum—a truth which the leaders of the Soviet Union never forgot. When they looked at the land masses on both their western and eastern flanks, they saw nations that were laid low by physical devastation, that were torn from within by bitter recriminations over the share of war guilt to be ascribed to various social classes, and by equally bitter rivalries over the right of access to the levers of power. The Soviet Union thus began a systematic effort to intrude itself into this vacuum, to bring whole peoples and vast resources within the Soviet orbit, and to do this by subversion from within and physical harassment from without.

When the implications of this development were grasped, the result was a profound wrench. Like a runner from Mara- thon, we had reached the last hill before Athens bearing news of a great victory—only to find that Athens has mysteriously

moved another 26 miles away, that for all the stabbing pain
the run must be resumed.

Five main lines of policy have characterized our renewal of
the run. First, in recognition of the division of the world into
East and West, has been the policy of military power and
strategic alliances known as containment. The second has been
our backing of a United Europe as the chosen instrument of
that policy. Third has been our effort to help the peoples of
Asia, Africa, and Latin America over the hump of misery into
the modern age of plenty. Fourth has been our determination
to make our own economy fulfill its promise of maximum employment, production, and purchasing power. And fifth has
been our resolve to end the shame of racial discrimination
within our society.

Let us now examine the development of these five major
themes, and how it came about that by 1963 we found ourselves wondering whether the last leg of the race was not much
longer and more difficult than we had thought.

A world divided

In the jargon of political science, the postwar world became
bipolar. One great cluster of peoples and resources centered
around the United States, an opposing cluster around the
Soviet Union. Bipolarization seemed as unchangeable as the
Alps. In an otherwise uncertain world, it became the fixed
reference point for all details of policy that marked the Cold
War, with its ebb and flow of crises and its omnipresent threat
of destruction.

On our side, whether we recognized it or not, the old dividing line between domestic and foreign affairs had become as
indistinct as a line drawn in water. What we did at home determined whether or not we would have the material resources
and the moral authority to do what needed to be done abroad.
What had to be done abroad, conversely, worked in its own

way to determine what we could do or had to do at home. In a sense every American—the man on the street, the Congressman, the President—became members of two constituencies: the voting one which went with their American citizenship, and the one representing other free people whose own actions affected and were affected by what Americans did. On the Soviet side, meanwhile, domestic and foreign affairs were never divisible. The peoples gathered up within the Soviet empire were brought firmly under the central control of Russia, and what was allowed to them or demanded of them in their internal life took its measure from what the Soviet rulers felt could best serve their own interests as the managers and chief beneficiaries of that empire.

So passed the late Forties and the Fifties. We are now well into the Sixties. It is, to be sure, always dangerous to attempt to lip-read history's meanings, and to assume that one can preempt her developments. We forearm ourselves against our own illusions, and hence against the shock of an eventual disillusion, if we remember always that the first law of history is the law of surprise. Nonetheless, if we are not altogether certain that the new era which seems to be dawning will not prove a false dawn, the evidence of our senses now tells us this much at least: that the halves of a world divided between a Soviet bloc and a Western bloc are each being rent from within by internal disputes and by tendencies that point to the rise of multiple power centers.

On the Soviet side, there has been the clash between the Russian and the Chinese Communist hierarchs. At issue here is the insistence of the Chinese that only through violence can the world-wide victory of communism be assured—as against the Russian insistence that victory is best assured by economic and political means where possible, by subversion and other mischief where necessary, but not by actions that might provoke a Western reaction with nuclear arms. More profoundly, it is an old-fashioned imperialist clash for land and spheres of influence, marked by racial antagonisms, by jealousies between the haves and the have-nots, by the reluctance of the Russian Communists to hold back a rise in living standards for their own people in order to provide developmental capital for their Chinese brethren—or to divert to the use of those brethren the Russian capital now being exported to non-Chinese Communist users.

While this clash among the Communist giants goes on, the satellite figures in the Communist world, from motives of their own, are reshuffling their positions. Poland is increasingly open to Western ideas and practices in matters from faith to farming. Albania has left the Soviet bloc for China. Rumania, for the moment, increasingly says "no" to Moscow and lives to tell the tale.

Further, the rumblings within the Communist bloc have been heard in the politics of Southern Asia, with consequences that are as yet indistinct. Provisionally, at least, the Chinese attack on India—apparently in defiance of a Russian veto—has brought India closer to the West, while Pakistan, in a countervailing reaction to the Indian move, has made tentative overtures to China.

We are entitled to think that the discord now heard in what used to be the monotoned Communist world reflects a Communist failure to manage their affairs so that each part of their world will contribute to and draw strength from the whole of it.

De Gaulle's challenge

The many voices that now challenge United States leadership in European affairs attest in their own way to the quality of that leadership since World War II. It was never our aim to make satellites out of our European friends. Our aim was to help restore them to health and to emancipate them from morbid fears, and so enable them once again to be the self-directed authors of their own history. Divorced from all else, therefore, we would be right in saying happily that we have attained our aim when we see France and Germany embarking on actions contrary to the lines of policy we would wish them to follow.

Yet to say this is to resemble the Englishman who, on being told that there were 10,000 pickpockets in London, responded proudly: "How marvelous, that the city of London should be so rich that it can provide so many pickpockets with pockets to pick!" The truth is, that for all our success in helping to reinvigorate the individual nations of Europe, we have seen that the ancient dream of a united Europe, the ambition of Charlemagne, Dante, and Henri V, cannot be unconditionally the goal of our foreign policy.

We had revived that dream to promote the economic recovery of Europe, to build a durable bridge of amity between the Germans and the French, to liquidate other envenoming national rivalries, and to enlarge Europe's power to share with the United States the costs of the Cold War struggle. The creation by the Six—France, Germany, Italy, Belgium, the Netherlands, and Luxembourg—of the Coal and Steel Community and the Common Market were significant steps toward these objectives.

But the very success of the Six raised the transcendent question of how Europe's emerging strength would be used—for proud, self-reliant, constructive cooperation with the rest of the free world, or for inward-looking, go-it-alone regionalism?

Our answer to this question has been the concept of "partnership"—the "dumbbell" theory that a strong United States and a strong united Europe would be the best basis of cooperative action.

Thus the United States said to the industrialized nations of Europe that it would move ahead toward partnership with Europe just as soon as a united Europe was achieved. This was the sense of the speech by McGeorge Bundy, Foreign Policy Adviser to the President, to the Economic Club of Chicago on Dec. 6, 1961:

It would be better if Western Europe were one great power. . . . My own belief is that the most productive way of conceiving the political future of the Atlantic community is to think in terms of a partnership between the United States on the one hand and a great European power on the other.

This same timetable—first a united Europe, then an Atlantic partnership—appeared in President Kennedy's July 4, 1962, speech at Independence Hall in Philadelphia:

The nations of Western Europe, long divided by feuds more bitter than any which existed among the thirteen colonies, are joining together, seeking as our forefathers sought to find freedom in diversity and unity in strength.

The United States looks on this vast new enterprise with hope and admiration. We do not regard a strong and united Europe as a rival but as a partner. To aid its progress has been the basic objective of our foreign policy for seventeen years. We believe that a united Europe will be capable of playing a greater role in the common defense, of responding more generously to the needs of poorer nations, of joining with the United States and others in lowering trade barriers, resolving problems of currency and commodities, and developing coordinated policies in all other economic, diplomatic and political areas. We see in such a Europe a partner with whom we could deal on a basis of full equality in all the great and burdensome tasks of building and defending a community of free nations.

It would be premature at this time to do more than indicate the high regard with which we view the formation of this partnership. The first order of business is for our European friends to go forward in forming the more perfect union which will some day make this partnership possible.

A great new edifice is not built overnight. It was eleven years from the Declaration of Independence to the writing of the Constitution. The construction of workable federal institutions required still another generation. The greatest works of our nation's founders lay not in documents and declarations, but in creative, determined action. The building of the new house of Europe has followed this same practical and purposeful course. Building the Atlantic partnership will not be cheaply or easily finished.

But I will say here and now on this day of independence that the United States will be ready for a Declaration of Interdependence—that we will be prepared to discuss with a United Europe the ways and means of forming a concrete Atlantic Partnership—a mutually beneficial partnership between the new union now emerging in Europe and the old American union founded here 175 years ago.

All this will not be completed in a year, but let the world know it as our goal.

This theory of partnership requires the United States to concentrate on the promotion of European unity as the first step toward broader action. But whether the theory is valid in other respects or not, it required us to remain largely immobile while European unity remained incomplete.

That this was a fatal defect was garishly exposed on Jan. 14, 1963, when Charles de Gaulle vetoed Great Britain's entry into the Common Market, thereby frustrating a European unity broader than the Six. Moreover, even progress toward greater unity among the present members of the European Economic Community fell under the dark shadow of De Gaulle's philosophy, according to which the EEC must be inward-looking and—at least agriculturally—autarchic, or it must disappear.

As for the Common Market, . . . it is of course the agricultural problem that the Six have still to settle. What would the very words "European Economic Community" mean if Europe did not for the most part assure its food supplies from its own agricultural products, which are amply sufficient for this? Indeed, the date adopted for the completion of the [agricultural] regulations still pending is December 31 [1963] . . . for the reason that the tariff negotiations between the United States and Europe are due to open next spring and that in face of the storms which will not fail to come upon that occasion, it will be necessary then that the Common Market be standing on its feet, complete and assured, or that it disappear.*

Accompanying this were his doubts about America's determination to defend Europe, his insistence on developing an independent nuclear force, his refusal to reconsider the reductions he had ordered in the French contribution to NATO's forces.

Seen in the light of 1963, our policy of "no European unity, no United States action," seemed sterile. The unity of Europe, or even of the six member nations of the Common Market, receded still further from reach.

Not even a bootstrap

Throughout most of the postwar period, the United States gave political support to the aspiration of colonial peoples for independence. Beyond this, we provided economic and technical assistance to both the old and new underdeveloped nations in their quest for a higher standard of living. Asian, Latin-American, and African countries have all been beneficiaries, just as a war-torn Europe once was.

Yet today, we are torn with doubts about our aid program. The problems presently afflicting it are largely the result of the vastness of the challenge and the slow pace of progress when, in so many places, even the bootstrap was missing by which people could lift themselves. After more than ten years of foreign aid, the average income of a citizen of the underdeveloped world—some $100 a year—remains about what it was. The growth in population has effectively swallowed up the intervening growth in income. At the same time, it has become clear that we have failed to fashion our policies on

* Charles de Gaulle, news conference, July 29, 1963.

an effective program of trade and international payments so as to promote growth in the new nations. Neither have we adequately mobilized the resources of the industrialized nations of the free world to build a more effective program of aid.

Jobs dwindle, growth dawdles

With the enactment of the Employment Act of 1946, we made full employment without inflation an avowed objective of national policy. Compared to the boom-and-bust cycles of the interwar period, we had reason to congratulate ourselves on our economic performance in the years that immediately followed the end of World War II. Instead of the acute depression that was widely predicted, we saw the seemingly fanciful figure of "60 million jobs" projected by Henry Wallace become, in fact, 70 million men and women gainfully employed. The bite of hardship was eased by the New Deal's "automatic stabilizers" of unemployment compensation, social security, and minimum wages.

Meanwhile, our economy kept growing at a respectable rate and at fairly high levels of employment in filling the pent-up demands of the war years, and meeting the requirements of the military buildup and of a Europe whose industrial machine was temporarily inoperative. These were the years of the acute dollar shortage for Europeans. These were the years in which America had most of the free world's productive capacity. These, in short, were the years when only "foreigners" had balance-of-payments problems.

These years are over. Western Europe's mighty industrial capacity has been reborn. Our rate of growth has slowed, and since 1958 our rate of unemployment has hovered at around 6 per cent of the total work force. Rather than a dollar gap, we have faced a persistent balance-of-payments deficit. The economic world all around us no longer has the shape of a

seller's market in which a horde of hungry buyers looks to us
as the principal supplier of the goods they want. It is a world
full of new competitors, with modern machines capable of
producing products that compete hard against our own even
in fields once thought preempted for the American factory
and the American worker.

It is now becoming clear that a more aggressive attack is in
order if there is to be any easing of our unemployment and
payments problems.

The Negro: freedom now!

Closely related to the considerations of the economy has been
the manner of our approach to America's greatest human
problem—the problem of guaranteeing and protecting the
rights of the Negro as a human being and as a citizen. Since
the end of World War II, we have in fact made measurable
progress in civil rights. But only men who embrace a policy
of willful blindness will say that the remedial actions have
been pressed with all the urgency that the seriousness of the
Negro grievances demand. Many Americans, including President Eisenhower, believed that progress in human rights must
come not through law, but through a change in the hearts
of men. The modest 1957 civil rights bill did not seriously
depart from this view.

But at last the patience of Negroes and of many white civil
rights advocates is exhausted. On the one hand, there are the
increasing number of demonstrations against racial discrimination; on the other, wholly disaffected Negroes going over to
Negro separatist movements such as the Black Muslims.
Clearly, the policy of gradualism in civil rights is among the
postwar policies that have gone bankrupt.

The problems we face in the middle years of the 1960's are
obviously complicated and seemingly intractable. It seems safe

to say that the process of division and subdivision of the bipolar world is only beginning. We cannot yet gauge what will happen if and when Red China, for example, becomes a significant nuclear power. Nor can we as yet foresee the consequences of further development by the United States and the Soviet Union of their military technology. Surely the Administration's efforts to ease East-West tension—as in the nuclear test ban—are welcome developments. And the same can be said about its efforts to secure from the Congress a greater right of discretion in dealing with such dissident Communist states as Yugoslavia and Poland. Yet in anything that touches on East-West relations, it will be some time before we can even begin to consider lowering our guard to any significant extent.

Meanwhile, in our relations with our Western Allies, we have not yet designed new policies to fit changed circumstances. In matters of trade and international payments, we have continued to defer excessively to our goal of establishing European unity on the foundation of the Common Market. Instead of reappraising our international relationships and adopting policies not encumbered by obeisance to an institution which has already accomplished the aims for which American support was initially given, we continue our narrowminded emphasis on support for the Six and its geographical expansion.

A month after De Gaulle ordained that Britain would for the foreseeable future remain outside the Market and that Europe would remain divided between the Six and the rest of Europe, Undersecretary of State George W. Ball, in a Feb. 15, 1963, letter to the Congressional Joint Economic Committee, reiterated as the first point in our United States policy toward Europe:

First, we shall continue to encourage the development of European unity and to express the hope that arrangements may ultimately be made for the accession of Great Britain to full membership in the EEC. Recent events have demonstrated a substantial body of European opinion in favor of Britain's participation in a united Europe, and the British Government has made known its own desire that the United Kingdom should play a full role in this development.

Our foreign aid program was subjected to new attacks at home. Most serious were the recommendations of the Clay Committee, headed by General Lucius Clay, which undercut the President's request for foreign aid appropriations. It should be said, however, that the program gained new strength in two ways. The first was the appointment of Budget Director David Bell, one of the brightest and best administrators of the New Frontier, as Administrator of the Agency for International Development. The second was the evolution of new criteria for the aid program, designed to focus aid on those countries which were doing most to erect progressive economic and social structures, and hence make our aid productive.

New initiatives were forthcoming in 1963 to speed the growth of our economy and cut down unemployment. President Kennedy proposed a tax cut to this end. A year before, the Trade Expansion Act was passed as a means of expanding the economy through the benefits of greater world trade.

Yet, America is still plagued by its balance-of-payments deficit—spending and investing more abroad than we take in. In 1963 European central bankers advised us to retard increases in our domestic supply of credit, and to raise interest rates in order to check outward flows of capital. This we did. The President coupled the interest rate increase with a proposed tax to discourage foreign borrowings, a decision to use our borrowing rights in the International Monetary Fund, and other proposals to live with and solve the payments deficit.

But the foundation needed to provide the 22 million new jobs the Sixties will require had not yet been laid.

In response to the cry for an end to racism, the President used the influence of his office and proposed to the Congress a program for securing to Negroes their rights in voting, education, public accommodations, and employment. It was the most comprehensive and far-reaching program ever proposed by an American President. Its importance is fundamental. As Harry Ashmore, the Pulitzer Prize-winning former editor of the *Arkansas Gazette,* said: "We can't get on with the nation's urgent business until we have begun, at least, to take care of the Negroes' needs."

President Kennedy's action was a brilliant beginning.

To compile the foregoing inventory of things that are awry is not to suggest that nothing can be done to set them right. It is rather to say that the watershed events of 1963 have sharpened our understanding of the central problems that confront us. Recognizing a problem is always an essential first step toward solving it.

As a progressive Democrat and a supporter of the Kennedy–Johnson program, I am interested in peace, national independence, humane institutions and civil liberties, equality and civil rights—both here and abroad.

My work in Congress has been particularly concerned with the economic buttresses of these broad objectives—with the questions of world trade, international payments, foreign aid, and full employment without inflation at home. As a member of the Joint Economic Committee, I have been privileged to study all these problems in the light of how they affect our national destiny. From this perspective I believe that we can frame an effective action program for Americans.

The goal of such a program is a free world community in which the industrialized members dedicate themselves to full employment without inflation, expanded trade, stable international payments, and long-term aid in partnership with the developing world.

As a politician, I realize that politics is indeed the art of the possible. My purpose, therefore, is to set forth specific, realizable programs for areas which, in my judgment, hold the key to the attainment of a free world community.

The community I envision would be open-ended. The only requirement for membership would be adherence to the principles of human freedom and dignity, shared economic progress, and peace. The members would be the industrialized nations of North America and Western Europe, together with Australia, New Zealand and Japan. The problems of providing aid, attaining full employment, and erecting a durable system of payments are of primary, though not exclusive, concern to these advanced industrialized nations. Likewise, these nations account for most of the world's trade and must act in concert to shape it in the interest of the whole free world.

The developing countries would be equal members of the community. Similarly, the way could be held open for many countries now Communist if future political events should allow their participation.

Regional groupings such as the Common Market or the European Free Trade Association could continue their progress toward more perfect union within the larger grouping. But they should not be allowed to prevent its formation.

By its nature, a free world community united for the economic and social benefit of all could provide a binding force that would hold the free world together despite the weakening of older ties based upon military or political foundations.

Such a free world community would naturally lead to subordination of NATO and some of our other alliances, though our military commitments and defenses would remain firm. But military needs alone are not enough on which to found a community. To the extent that we find it possible to de-emphasize our military alliances, it will be less damaging to free world morale when France (or the next country) withdraws troops from the alliance, or insists on developing its own separate nuclear force. A program that would provide a firm new basis for Western unity could mitigate the frustration and danger of temporary expedients (such as the multilateral nuclear force) to shore up old unities.

A free world community will require large changes in our present policies for world trade, international payments, development aid, and growth and employment. In chapters 2 through 6, I attempt to set out the nature of some of these changes.

A community such as I envisage will require a political organization more effective than the mere sporadic cooperation of nation-states. But it would serve no purpose to set up an over-all rump "Free World United Nations" of the developed and the developing countries. What *is* vital is a method of mobilizing the strength of the developed countries for the benefit of the whole free world. For this purpose, we need a radical upgrading of the existing Organization for Economic Cooperation and Development, by adding to it a commission to propose, a parliamentary conference to debate, and a ministerial council to act, as described in Chapter 7.

Such measures can be translated into reality here only through our institutions of the Presidency and the Congress.

Clearly, the vast agenda of a free world community requires a President cast in the mold of Jefferson, Lincoln, and Franklin Delano Roosevelt—one who will formulate comprehensive programs, educate the people in their substance, and work with Congress as an equal participant in the legislative process.

Professor James MacGregor Burns has outlined the qualities of such a presidential leader:

He must gain leadership of a big national party and guide it in seizing and holding majority status. He must publicize his and his party's program and goals with such clarity and conviction that he can help convert latent and amorphous popular attitudes into a powerful public opinion bolstering his cause. He must build structural support in his personal following by merging it with his national party organization or by creating new political units. He must keep his party eternally competitive and thus fulfill the first requirements of the Jeffersonian strategy. He must be willing to narrow his personal popularity if by so doing he can intensify and consolidate a working majority in Congress or the electorate. He must be willing in emergencies to take sweeping action, no matter how controversial, and then to appeal to the electorate for a majority, as Jefferson did in 1804 after the Louisiana Purchase, and Roosevelt in 1940 after the destroyer deal with the British.

The presidential leader must, in short, be more than a skillful manipulator or brilliant interpreter. He must be a constructive innovator, who can reshape to some degree the constellation of political forces in which he operates. To reach the acme of leadership he must achieve a creative union of intellectual comprehension, strategic planning, and tactical skill, to a degree perhaps not paralleled since Jefferson." *

But even a President who follows this concept of leadership is doomed to frustration unless he is given a Congress which is at once independent, strong, and responsive to great issues.

In short, the institution of our government which needs strengthening and reforming is the Congress. It is the place, according to Sen. Joseph Clark of Pennsylvania:

. . . where the vested interest lobbies run riot, where conflict of interest rides unchecked, where demagoguery knows few bounds, where political lag keeps needed action a generation behind the times, where the 19th century reigns supreme in committees, where ignorance is often at a premium and wisdom at a discount, where the evil influence of arrogant and corrupt political machines ignores most successfully the public interest, where the lust for patronage and favors for the faithful do the greatest damage to the public interest.

Congress cannot perform the tasks that will be asked of it until it accurately reflects the will of the broad body of our citizens, fairly districted; until it permits the great issues to come before it for a straightforward vote; until it leavens the

* *The Deadlock of Democracy* (1963), pp. 337–338.

lump of the seniority system to prevent rule by the few; until it lightens the administrative workload on its legislators so as to give them time enough to think out the great substantive decisions.

This will mean extension of the franchise and an end to gerrymandered districts. This will mean reform of the House Rules Committee to remove its present power to bottle up legislation, and change in the Senate's Rule 22 so as to end the power of endless delay by filibuster. It will mean, at the least, buffing the rough edges of the seniority system by letting the majority of a committee work its will despite a recalcitrant chairman. It will mean evolving new devices to free a Congressman or Senator from the tyranny of casework. All these matters are discussed in Chapter 8.

CHAPTER TWO

Our Trade Policy:
Out from a Tight Corner

So, in the Libyan fable it is told
That once an eagle, stricken with a dart,
Said, when he saw the fashion of the shaft,
"With our own feathers, not by other's hand,
Are we now smitten."   Aeschylus

On all sides nowadays we hear talk of how the strength of the American eagle—the symbol of the American dollar—is threatened by serious and continuing deficits in our international balance of payments. On all sides, too, we hear that a marked increase in our export trade will go far toward removing those deficits. But we hear little about the central question: Have we tried to remove all barriers to our exports, or have we in fact helped *raise* those barriers against ourselves?

Almost two centuries ago Adam Smith gave the classical justification of free trade—that we export in order to obtain the advantages to us of goods and services produced abroad.

The advantages of imports are obvious in the case of goods and services unavailable at home or obtainable only at very high cost. We cannot supply our needs for coffee, bananas, or cultured pearls through domestic production. In the nature of things, a trip to Europe cannot be taken by staying at home.

But the advantages of exporting in order to import are equally important in the case of goods produced by both trading partners. World trade allows each country to specialize in

20

those products in which it is most efficient. Consumers gain by being able to choose among a variety of articles. Producers are stimulated to improve their own products or to develop new ones. This happened, for example, when the major American automobile manufacturers developed compact cars in response to heavy imports of small cars from Europe. In this case, the consumer, having the choice between American and European compacts, then chose increasingly to buy the American versions.

If we were concerned mainly with the normal commercial items in our balance of payments (the exchange of goods and services, a reasonable amount of foreign travel, and a reasonable volume of capital investment abroad), our present merchandise export surplus of about $4 billion per year—the difference between $20 billion exports and $16 billion imports—would seem more than adequate.

But export earnings, together with other sources of international income, fail by an annual average of around $3 billion to pay for our actual foreign expenditures, mainly worldwide defense, foreign aid, and private capital investments abroad. The latter include direct investment—Procter and Gamble builds a detergent plant in Germany, and portfolio investment—an American investor purchases shares on the Stock Exchange in a Dutch electronics firm. While we can and should curtail some types of foreign expenditures temporarily, the long-run solution to our balance-of-payments problem can best be found in a further expansion of exports.

No other single source of our international receipts—tourism, capital inflow (as when Bowater of Britain builds a plant in Tennessee, or a French investor buys General Motors stock), earnings on foreign investment—even approaches the magnitude of exports. Two-thirds of our receipts from foreign sources come from our merchandise exports. In 1962, our entire payments deficit was $2.2 billion. Exports of goods came to a bit over $20 billion. A 10 per cent increase in exports, therefore, would have very nearly wiped out the deficit. By comparison, we would have had to triple our earnings on foreign tourism in America to eliminate the deficit.

While eliminating our international imbalance, export expansion can also help the domestic economy. We have a great deal of unused capacity and a high rate of unemployment. Putting some of the idle men and factories to work producing for export would increase incomes and provide a continuing stimulus to the domestic economy. Moreover, if we create a good general climate for export expansion, the most efficient American industries are the ones most likely to increase foreign sales. These are just the industries which can provide a sound basis for domestic economic expansion.

Recognizing the need for expanded exports, we passed the Trade Expansion Act of 1962. We empowered the Export-Import Bank to embark upon a multibillion-dollar program of insuring American exporters against defaults by their purchasers. We revived E Awards for outstanding export performance by American industry. We exhorted our business leaders to get out and sell in world markets.

But United States exports have so far risen slowly, and the deficit in our international payments still persists.

Why?

The astonishing answer, which comes out clearly from a study of our trade policy since World War II, is that we have in fact helped to set up discriminatory trading areas which present formidable obstacles to our maintaining, much less increasing, our export surplus. This self-defeating line of action was not deliberate. It was a consequence of an overriding emphasis on the integration of Europe that distorted our world trade policy.

How our policy on European integration came to triumph over our policy on world trade

The two greatest obstacles to expanded United States exports are the two enormous preferential trading blocs in Europe: the Common Market (the Six) of France, West Germany, Italy, Belgium, the Netherlands, and Luxembourg; and the European Free Trade Association (the Seven) of the United Kingdom, Norway, Denmark, Sweden, Austria, Switzerland, Portugal, and (as an associate) Finland. Both are reducing tariffs within their respective areas, but denying non-member countries these privileges. In addition, the Common Market is establishing a common external tariff around the Six which has the effect of increasing tariffs in former low-tariff countries such as the Netherlands and Germany, where we have done the most business. For this reason, the Common Market is the more injurious to our export interests. It is the Common Market which we have most assiduously supported. What follows is an account of how we managed to arrive at such a conflict in our trade policy.

THE HEYDAY OF MULTILATERALISM (1945–47)

The end of World War II saw us determined to set the world on the high road of free and multilateral trade and payments, and away from the shambles we inherited from two world wars, a terrible depression, and rampant economic nationalism. High tariffs, discriminatory quotas, blocked currencies and bilateral bartering characterized not only Hjalmar Schacht's Germany, but in some degree most countries in the world.

Multilateralism was the watchword of the two great free world economic agencies which we helped to found. Under the International Monetary Fund, launched at Bretton Woods in 1944, the foundation was laid for monetary stability and orderly adjustment of exchange rates. Exchange controls on current transactions, making it impossible to get money out of a country, and quota restrictions were made illegal unless a country was in balance-of-payments trouble.

Under the General Agreement on Tariffs and Trade, signed by 24 countries at Geneva in 1947, quotas were likewise made illegal except for countries with balance-of-payments deficits. Tariffs were to be bargained down gradually in multilateral tariff negotiations on an unconditional, most-favored-nation basis. Most-favored-nation treatment means that if country A reduces its tariff on, say, typewriters to country B, it must extend the same reduction to other countries. A country that receives such treatment is thus assured that it will not be discriminated against.

GATT's founders envisaged that it would be replaced by a permanent International Trade Organization. However, because the United States would not agree to formal membership in the ITO because of fears about "sovereignty," the "temporary" GATT has continued to be the means for world-wide tariff reductions.

A TASTE OF DISCRIMINATION (1948–52)

The Marshall Plan days. Soon after the establishment of IMF and GATT, it became apparent that they alone could not restore a Europe still prostrate from the war. Europe was drained of monetary resources; production rose slowly; trade languished; and commerce threatened to slip back into bilateral patterns.

The Marshall Plan, first presented in Secretary of State George Marshall's Harvard speech of June, 1947, and enacted in April, 1948, was a program of massive United States aid to enable Europe to regain economic health. In General Marshall's speech there was scarcely a hint of American backing for European integration. Indeed, Marshall Plan aid was originally offered to East European as well as West European countries, and to the separate West European countries after its rejection by East Europe. We did, however, insist that the participating countries assist in the allocation of the aid funds.

The Organization for European Economic Cooperation, established by the Western European countries to help allocate Marshall Plan funds, set itself the broader objective of increasing European trade. Its early activity to this end was a program of eliminating intra-European quotas which restricted imports.

The United States, on its part, acquiesced in the idea that the European countries could discriminate in their trade by removing quotas on the shipment of goods among themselves, while retaining quotas on United States imports. This was entirely legal under GATT, since nearly all the European countries were in deficit to the United States.

The program for removing the internal quotas of the OEEC countries foundered, because countries in deficit in their international payments with other countries within OEEC dared not remove the quotas for fear of increasing their deficits. Unless the problem of financing these deficits could be solved, therefore, trade could not increase. To meet this problem, the OEEC in 1949 set up the European Payments Union, enabling deficit countries to pay for a part of their deficits with credit provided by the Union. The United States approved, and backed it up with a $350-million capital contribution to the Union. The EPU, like the internal removal of OEEC quotas, was on a regional basis and discriminatory; but we recognized that Western Europe's problems of reconstruction justified temporary discrimination against outsiders.

Freeing Europe's trade: from multilateralism to regionalism. In the early days of the Marshall Plan there was some talk in OEEC of studying the possibility of further customs unions and free trade areas * in Europe, possibly along the lines of

---

* Customs unions and free trade areas both provide for the elimination of tariffs among their members. The former sets up a common external tariff against outsiders; the latter allows member countries to set their own individual external tariffs.

Benelux, the Belgium-Netherlands-Luxembourg customs union set up in 1948. But the main European emphasis was still on lowering world-wide tariffs on a multilateral, nondiscriminatory, GATT basis.

The need for lower tariffs soon became obvious. As intra-European quotas on the movement of goods were progressively removed, it became apparent that low-tariff countries like those of Benelux and Scandinavia would be excellent markets for high-tariff countries like France and Italy, but that the high tariffs of the latter would hold back trade in the reverse direction. Accordingly, Belgium in 1951 proposed unilateral tariff reductions by the high-tariff European countries, to be applicable to all GATT members. High-tariff France responded, as might have been expected, by proposing a GATT agreement to reduce the tariffs of all countries by 30 per cent in three stages—again, on a free world-wide, rather than on a discriminatory European basis. The Council of Europe, established at Strasbourg in 1949, sponsored a plan to make GATT a "low tariff club," in which all free world countries would agree to work gradually toward much lower tariffs across the board. These hopeful beginnings were discussed long and hard in GATT at Geneva in 1951 and 1952.

Unfortunately, the Eisenhower Administration, on taking office in 1953, failed to support any of these proposals, and that was the end of them. Isaiah Frank, then Acting Director of the Office of International Trade in our State Department, relates the sad story of what happened:

> The main principles of the French Plan . . . [were] refined and developed in the course of two years of discussion in the GATT. . . .
>
> Unfortunately, the French Plan never really got off the ground. Because it embodied principles and raised policy issues of a sensitive domestic political character in a number of countries, a careful effort was made in the GATT to skirt around the basic issues in-

volved and to concentrate on "technical" studies and refinements of the Plan. Although Benelux and the Scandinavian countries looked upon it with favor, the high-tariff countries showed no enthusiasm for the automatic features of the Plan. So far as the United States was concerned, the Plan raised serious problems of legislative authority as well as of policy at a time when a new Administration had just come in and was in process of a full-scale review of existing trade policy. At the GATT session in October, 1953, therefore, the United States representative said that his government "intended to study the Plan carefully and that it would be sent to the Randall Commission [Commission on Foreign Economic Policy] to illustrate a line of thinking on the subject and a possible line of approach." The *Staff Papers* published by the Randall Commission include a brief summary of the French Plan among the descriptions of alternative possibilities for the delegation to the President of tariff-changing authority. Although the Plan was undoubtedly considered by the Commission, its final report contains no reference to it.*

Thus perished what might have been a promising program for substantial tariff reductions on a nondiscriminatory basis throughout the free world.

The Voice of America. Few voices were raised in America in those days warning of the dangers posed by a customs union to the GATT principle of nondiscrimination. Almost alone, Prof. Jacob Viner, that Olympian economist who served first at the University of Chicago and then at Princeton, warned prophetically of the dangers of a European customs union in 1950:

Should the movement for customs union in Western Europe make rapid progress, however, it should be the American position that all friendly European countries should receive invitations to participate on equitable terms. The economic future of any Euro-

* Isaiah Frank, *The European Common Market* (1961), pp. 19–21.

pean country which was left outside a Western European customs union and was also outside the Russian economic orbit would be grim indeed. Western European economic union would also result in there being left stranded unless rescued by the United States a number of non-European economic orphans. Whatever its merits, economic, political, strategic, moreover, Western European economic union launched under the inauspicious circumstances of open American pressures would carry forever a heavy burden of international unpopularity. . . .

For the long-run problem of raising the level of economic well-being for the peoples of the world in general, customs union is only a partial, uncertain, and otherwise imperfect means of doing what world-wide non-discriminatory reduction of trade barriers can do more fully, more certainly, and more equitably and it will be a sad outcome of confused thinking on our part if we in effect abandon our pursuit of the greater economic goal because of our fresh, and romantic, infatuation with the lesser goal.*

But most of us were less discerning than Professor Viner. Had not the United States of America become great because it was a continental free trade area? Would not reducing trade barriers between the countries of Europe lessen the aid burden on the American taxpayer? Had not America from the time of Washington's Farewell Address been plagued with quarrels between the European states? Why not a United States of Europe?

European integration was strongly supported by powerful voices in the United States. On March 22, 1947, resolutions were introduced in both Houses of Congress calling for a "United States of Europe." In May, 1947, Undersecretary of State for Economic Affairs William Clayton, in suggesting an American aid plan for European recovery, wrote:

Such a plan should be based on a European economic federation on the order of the Belgium-Netherlands-Luxembourg Customs Union. Europe cannot recover from this war and again become

* Jacob Viner, *The Customs Union Issue* (1950), pp. 133–135.

independent if her economy continues to be divided into many small watertight compartments as it is today.*

The preamble to the Foreign Assistance Act of 1948 expressed the sense of Congress as favoring for Europe "a large domestic market with no internal trade barriers."

Both within the State Department and the Economic Cooperation Administration, set up to administer the Marshall Plan, there were strong adherents of the view that European economic unification was essential. None was so outspoken as ECA Administrator Paul Hoffman, who told the OEEC Ministerial Council in Paris on Oct. 1, 1949, that a common market should be formed with all OEEC countries included. The State Department, less enthusiastic than ECA, was responsible for striking the word "unification" from Hoffman's draft speech and substituting "integration."

Meanwhile, at the Havana Conference in 1948, the United States agreed to except customs unions and free trade areas from the general GATT rule against the discriminatory lowering of tariff barriers.

The European Coal and Steel Community.   Meanwhile, two different movements toward integration were converging in Europe. One envisaged a supranational political authority which would gradually extend its jurisdiction over areas of common interest. The other, concentrating on economic integration, envisaged proceeding commodity by commodity or function by function to a customs union. In 1950, Jean Monnet, then head of the French planning organization, proposed, and France's Foreign Minister, Robert Schuman, carried through, an amalgamation of these two approaches to unity: the Schuman Plan for a coal and steel customs union. The plan was largely a political device (1) to permit the reconstruction of West German heavy industry under other than exclusively

* Quoted in Max Beloff, *The United States and the Unity of Europe* (1963), p. 20.

German control, and (2) to lay the foundation for a future united Europe. Britain was invited to join the group. Because Britain's insularity still dominated the public mind, and because Labour feared outside interference with the nationalized steel industry, it declined. Thus the membership of the European Coal and Steel Community (ECSC) was confined to France, Germany, Italy, Belgium, the Netherlands, and Luxembourg—subsequently the Six of the Common Market.

There was an important legal hitch to the aspirations of the ECSC for a discriminatory trade area—one which eliminated tariffs within the group but established common tariffs for outsiders—for two commodities, coal and steel. The GATT exemption from the general rule of nondiscriminatory, most-favored-nation treatment permitted customs unions and free trade areas only on a substantially across-the-board basis, not just on a few individual commodities. The Six approached the GATT humbly, promising if a waiver were granted to set their external duties on coal and steel "upon a basis which shall be lower and less restrictive than the general incidence of the duties and regulations of commerce now applicable"— in other words to compensate the rest of the world for the special privilege of discrimination sought by the Six. The GATT finally granted ECSC's request for a waiver in November, 1952. But as it stated in its annual report, the GATT Secretariat clearly saw the possible conflict of these new regional proposals with the fundamental principles of GATT:

It is evident that we have entered upon a period when governments are giving serious consideration to plans for economic integration involving the modification or suspension of commitments under the General Agreement. They may be tempted to neglect contractual obligations. All new regional schemes in Europe or elsewhere will have to be thoroughly examined in the light of the obligations of the contracting parties. New problems require new solutions, and if the General Agreement is to continue as a significant factor in international affairs, solutions must be found which will not disturb the essential elements and principles of the Agreement.*

The ECSC marked the first step to create a "supranational" authority in Europe. Its machinery includes the High Authority, composed of individuals chosen for competence and uninstructed by their governments, who exercise decision-making power like that of a domestic legislature, including the power to tax, borrow, and lend; and the Common Assembly, which has power to overturn the High Authority. The ECSC has the power to conduct international relations with other states.

The plan for ECSC was proposed by the French government without prior consultation with the United States. It was pointed out that the ECSC was inconsistent with expressed United States policy of support for reunification of East and West Germany. But the United States government speedily discarded whatever standoffish attitude there was toward European integration. Shortly after it was proposed in 1950, ECSC was endorsed by Secretary of State Dean Acheson, ECA Administrator Paul Hoffman, and President Truman. The Pentagon, which wanted German rearmament, also backed ECSC, particularly when the French insisted in September, 1950, that the Schuman Plan negotiation must be concluded before any action on German rearmament.

Congress, too, supported the ECSC, providing in the Mutual Security Act of 1952 for assistance to be given directly to the ECSC. It hoped that ECSC, by augmenting European strength, would allow reduction of United States aid to Europe.

Americans played an important role in drafting the six-nation treaty and securing its ratification. High Commissioner to Germany John McCloy helped overcome opposition in Germany, as did his General Counsel Robert Bowie, who was later to become Chief of Secretary of State Dulles' Policy Planning Staff. In the United States, George Ball, now Undersecretary

* *GATT in Action,* Third Report on the Operation of the General Agreement on Tariffs and Trade (Geneva, January, 1952), pp. 28–29.

of State, became consultant to the French government on the treaty. The treaty was signed on March 19, 1951, and ratification was completed by June 1, 1952.

OUR TRADE POLICY SUBORDINATED
TO EUROPEAN INTEGRATION (1953–60)

Further support for the Coal and Steel Community.   When John Foster Dulles took office as Secretary of State in January, 1953, our support for the ECSC became more vigorous than ever. Dulles had long been an advocate of European political unity, and he shared the hopes of ECSC's founders that it was a promising beginning toward that goal. He appointed an ambassador to the authority and got Congress to approve a $100-million loan to the organization.

The European Defense Community.   The Korean War, following upon the Prague *coup* and the Berlin blockade, generated fears of a Communist attack on Western Europe. The United States, in consequence, increased its support of European integration, shifting its emphasis to the need for increased European military strength. Thus NATO Commander Eisenhower became an exponent of European unity for the military advantages that it would confer. The Lisbon Conference of the NATO powers in 1952 set targets for the proposed NATO force on the ground in Europe that clearly could be fulfilled only by including German divisions. And the 1952 Mutual Security Act contained a renewed Congressional hint:

The Congress welcomes the recent progress in political federation, military integration and economic unification in Europe and reaffirms its belief in the necessity of further vigorous efforts toward these ends as a means of building strength, establishing security and preserving peace in the North Atlantic Area.

The original French proposal of 1950 for a European Defense Community (EDC) was for a European army in which only battalion-sized units could be exclusively German. Premier René Pleven, who advanced the proposal, wanted to prevent the formation of a large German army and yet to go along with German participation in a common European force.

America's support for EDC originally stemmed from a similar conviction that the defense of Western Europe required German troops, and that German military units could best be accommodated in a truly European Army. But General Eisenhower, speaking to the English-Speaking Union at London's Guildhall on July 23, 1951, appeared convinced that the Germans would rearm only if allowed a national army. American opinion came to favor the formation of sizable German units for inclusion as such under the EDC.

After Dulles became Secretary of State in January, 1953, American support for such an EDC increased immensely because he saw it as a basic instrument for European integration. At Secretary Dulles' instigation, extreme pressure was applied to the French in 1953 and 1954 to go along with an EDC which bore little resemblance to the original Pleven plan. Indeed, under Dulles' urging, Congress voted to allow the President to withhold up to $1 billion in American aid until the EDC came into effect. Nor was this all. In his "agonizing reappraisal" speech of Dec. 14, 1953, Dulles hinted that we would withdraw American aid to Europe unless the French bought the EDC proposal.

Understandably unhappy about both the substance of the American version of a European army and the pressure used to obtain it, the French rejected the EDC.

This setback was a blow to the United States campaign for European integration. Although we swallowed our pride and forgot about any "agonizing reappraisal" after the failure of EDC, we remained singularly unenthusiastic when the British-sponsored Western European Union safely brought German armed forces into NATO, on terms not vastly different from those we had been pressing for under our version of the EDC.

The Common Market. If one way of achieving European unity was barred by the demise of the EDC, there were others. The ECSC Six, at Messina in 1955, decided to approach the goal via a customs union. At the same time, plans were drawn up for the European Atomic Energy Community, which was then considered as the more likely vehicle for eventual political unity. The United States threw its decisive support behind the new project when President Eisenhower, in 1957, announced that we would allocate fuel to EURATOM as well as help in the construction of reactors to produce atomic energy for peaceful purposes.

Meanwhile, the Rome Treaty, setting up the European Economic Community of the Six—the Common Market— was signed in 1956 and ratified during 1957. Other members of GATT soon pointed out that the terms of the Rome Treaty were inconsistent with GATT principles, and that the treaty would be highly injurious to their trade and to the trade of all GATT members outside the preferential area.

The United States' official position could see no conflict between the Common Market and GATT objectives:

> Since the six countries are also participants in the General Agreement on Tariffs and Trade, it is assumed that such import restrictions as may be found necessary to maintain will be consistent with the standards of the general agreement.*

The other GATT members emphatically disagreed. They got together and submitted 132 questions to the Six on the compatibility of the proposed Common Market with GATT.†

These questions were the main business of the stormy twelfth session of GATT, which convened in Geneva in October and November, 1957, to discuss the Rome Treaty. Every major aspect of the treaty was challenged—the proposed

---

* Statement of U.S. official views, State Department Press Release #21, Jan. 15, 1957.

† *The Economist,* Oct. 19, 1957, p. 236.

method of averaging tariffs, the proposed dismantling of intra-European quotas on a discriminatory basis, the proposed common agriculture policy, and the French and Belgian proposal that their former colonies be accorded preferential treatment.*

The United States rose to the defense. Assistant Secretary of State Thomas C. Mann, head of the United States delegation, said on October 28, 1957:

Let us all recognize the fundamental fact that the General Agreement and the Rome Treaty have common and mutually reinforcing aims. . . . the Rome Treaty and the General Agreement . . . are companions on the road to improved economic relationships between nations and a better life for their peoples.†

But the other GATT members were not persuaded. The session adjourned with no agreement, and a special session had to be scheduled in 1958. At that 1958 session, the GATT members "decided to declare a truce on the question of the legal compatibility of the Treaty with the GATT, with the understanding that the indefinite postponement of these issues would not prejudice the rights of the Contracting Parties under Article XXIV." ‡

Meanwhile, there was widespread concern in Europe about how to prevent a split between the Six and the rest of Europe. The British, in 1956, proposed to the OEEC that a Free Trade Area on a Europe-wide basis be set up with the Common Market as a unit. The United States, the Six of the Common Market, and practically every other OEEC country initially supported the proposal. This was particularly true of Germany, with its extensive trade relations with Sweden, Denmark, Austria and Switzerland.

---

* Germany and the Netherlands at first objected to the French and Belgian proposal, but ultimately acquiesced, apparently as part of the price of French and Belgian participation in the Common Market.

† State Department Bulletin, Nov. 25, 1957, p. 846.

‡ Isaiah Frank, *The European Common Market* (1961), p. 164.

But presently the French, lucid and juridical, brought up objections. In a free trade area, each country keeps its own separate tariffs toward the rest of the world, while eliminating its tariffs toward other countries in the area. The absence of a common external tariff, said the French, would cause chaos. A low-tariff country like Sweden, by importing raw materials and components at low cost, could have an unfair advantage over countries like France whose costs were pushed up by high tariffs.*

Behind the negotiating façade, France undoubtedly suspected, with some justification, that Britain was trying to have her cake and eat it, too: to retain her British Commonwealth preferential area *and* get free trading rights in Europe.

When the De Gaulle government came to power in mid-1958, the French objection to the British proposal hardened. De Gaulle was not willing to see the infant Common Market of the Six drown in the large European sea. France vetoed the proposal in December, 1958.

With a Europe-wide free trade area dead, Britain then took the lead in founding the European Free Trade Association, based originally on Britain, Denmark, Norway, Sweden, Switzerland, and Austria. With the inclusion of Portugal, it became the "Outer Seven," with Finland soon added as an associate. EFTA set its timetable for the elimination of tariffs among its members to coincide with the Common Market's timetable.

The United States, which had approved the Europe-wide free trade area, was not very happy about EFTA. According to Professor Max Beloff of Oxford:

It was made very plain to the countries concerned that this grouping was not in the American view deserving of the approval

---

* In fact, this feature is what tends to make a free trade area a liberal device by inducing its high tariff members to lower their tariffs toward the rest of the world in order to compete within the free trade area.

that the activities of the Six elicited. Indeed, some overt hostility toward it was scarcely concealed.*

Dissenting American voices. Meanwhile, thoughtful American experts were warning of the dangers of emerging European regionalism.

Economist Raymond Vernon, formerly acting director of the Office of Economic and Trade Policy, Department of State, said at Haverford College in 1956:

> Unless these developments [European regional groupings] were somehow firmly subjected to the discipline of larger global groupings, there would seem to be a substantial possibility that the resulting European economic bloc could be oriented to a policy of substantial independence from—even conceivably an hostility to— the rest of the Atlantic Community . . . It would be risky to take anything for granted as to the trade policy of such a group toward the rest of the Atlantic Community.†

Professor Lincoln Gordon of Harvard, now American Ambassador to Brazil, said at the same conference:

> If the contemplated European integration is feasible, it should be in the framework of, not an Atlantic Community, but an orderly international system, to make sure that the relations of the Six . . . were not at the expense of their relations with the rest of the world.‡

Emile Despres, then chairman of the economics department at Williams College, told the Joint Economic Committee in June, 1959:

* Max Beloff, *The United States and the Unity of Europe* (1963), p. 95; see also Emile Benoit, *Europe at Sixes and Sevens* (1961), p. 95 on this point.

† Haviland (ed.), *The United States and the Western Community* (1957), p. 61.

‡ Lincoln Gordon, cited in *ibid.,* p. 143.

Since France and Italy have very high tariffs, Germany high tariffs and only Benelux has a low tariff, the broad formula for the common tariff proposed in the Treaty of Rome—an average of the present tariffs of member countries—would yield a highly disruptive degree of trade discrimination between members and nonmembers. An external tariff at any such level must be prevented.*

The House Foreign Affairs Committee's European Subcommittee, led by Rep. Frank Coffin of Maine (later deputy administrator, Agency for International Development), said:

As the United States prepares for the 1960 GATT negotiations at Geneva . . . it should press for a liberal external tariff for the Common Market, considerably lower than the result achieved by the arithmetic average.†

Padraic Frucht, economist and former minority staff consultant, Joint Economic Committee, said:

It is an unfortunate fact that the development of regional economic integration strikes at the bonds that tie together the free world as a whole while it is cementing the bonds among certain of its members. . . . While moving sideways on trade policy, the United States in supporting the EEC in effect turned from its traditional multilateralism. . . . By allowing the steam to go out of its drive toward multilateralism, the United States has unwittingly aided the Soviets. . . .‡

But despite these dissents, the general trend of the Eisenhower Administration was strongly pro-Common Market.

FURTHER DISTORTION
OF OUR TRADE POLICY (1961–63)

What would the coming to power of the Kennedy Administration do to United States policy toward the Common Mar-

* Joint Economic Committee Hearings, June–July, 1959, p. 1036.
† Report, House Committee on Foreign Affairs, Jan. 11, 1960, p. 88.
‡ *Congressional Record,* Feb. 7, 1962, p. 1794.

ket, and its expansion? Would the Dulles-Eisenhower policy be continued, or would voices urging reappraisal be heeded? Would we urge Britain to apply for membership, or would Britain's EFTA grouping be encouraged as a more serviceable way to the larger community of freely trading nations? Would the United States, by proposing a world-wide, nondiscriminatory new trade program, return from the paths of particularism to the highroad of multilateralism?

These questions were soon decisively answered when it became known who would be Undersecretary of State for Economic Affairs. This turned out to be George W. Ball, whose intellectual commitment to the Common Market went back many years. If anything, the Eisenhower pro-Common Market policy would be strengthened. Ball had often in the past tried to set to rest Congressional fears that the Common Market might substantially disadvantage the United States. Appearing before the Joint Economic Committee on July 1, 1959, for example, "in a purely private capacity," although "the law firm of which I am a member serves as the legal counsel in the United States for the Commission of the European Economic Community, and also for the High Authority of the European Coal and Steel Community," Ball had testified:

> I think that this apparent disadvantage has been overstated and that there has probably been too much concern in America over this question of disadvantage. . . . there are good reasons to believe that the Common Market will never have the psychology of a restrictive trading bloc. The treaty is explicit in requiring a liberal commercial policy, and it has been my observation that the men who have the responsibility at the moment for the administration of the treaty are determined to bring about a liberal attitude on the part of the Community.

"Newspeak" and "dangerous thoughts." George Orwell's *1984* describes the principles of "Newspeak," the official language in vogue in 1984. Its vocabulary "consisted of words

which had been deliberately constructed for political purposes: words, that is to say, which not only had in every case a political implication, but were intended to impose a desirable mental attitude upon the person using them." Something perilously close to Newspeak became the common parlance of the State Department. Normally, when tariffs are raised against us, Americans are not backward about calling things by their right names. The rise of a discriminatory trading area would be a "threat," not a "challenge" or an "opportunity." Engaging in tariff negotiations designed to reduce your opposite number's tariffs would be called "bargaining," not "partnership." The results of a tariff negotiation, if successful, would be announced as "tariff reductions," not as a "step toward Atlantic unity."

The fixation on the Common Market led to another practice on the part of the State Department. The Japanese government during World War II, it is said, forbade its people from having "dangerous thoughts." The State Department, too, must have been concerned about the consequences of "dangerous thoughts," like the possibility that the Common Market would not always be good for the United States. For example, it made no study of the effects of Common Market discrimination on United States exports until late in 1961. This study, made by the State Department's Bureau of Intelligence and Research, concluded that United States exports of manufactures and industrial materials to the Common Market (the Six plus Greece as an associate) would go down 9 to 9½ per cent when the proposed common external tariff was fully in effect. It went on to say that the expansion of the Common Market to include eight other European countries (the seven of EFTA plus Finland) would reduce our exports of manufactures and industrial materials by 11½ to 12½ per cent. It pointed out that we would incur additional losses in our agricultural exports. The study was never released to the public.

Further, despite the great significance of the Common Market's tariff schedule to this country, no government agency took the time and trouble to work out a comprehensive comparison of United States and Common Market tariffs, by translating our tariff descriptions to those used by the Common Market. In the face of this default by the government, the private Committee for Economic Development finally did the job; its two huge volumes, selling for $50, are at last available for our tariff negotiators and exporters.

We almost abort a trade bill. United States foreign economic policy developed a split personality in late 1961: at the same time we were both for and against tariff reduction. Our reciprocal trade program, in effect since the mid-Thirties, was scheduled to expire on June 30, 1962. Unless we wished to end a quarter-century of effort to bring about liberalized trade, the program had to be renewed. Also, however, the State Department very much wanted the Common Market enlarged by Britain's joining it. With Britain as a member, the Department hoped that the Common Market would be "outward-looking" and less likely to display "Little Europe" tendencies.*

If the United States were to propose world-wide tariff reductions under a new program to replace the expiring Reciprocal Trade Agreements Act, Britain might well consider that it

---

* With regard to the entry of Britain, the National Committee for an Effective Congress on Dec. 27, 1961, issued this version of the "Britain-must-join" argument:

"Today this simple truth is becoming apparent to Washington as well as to Wall Street: that a Europe organized without the United States would be a Europe organized against the United States. This is why we are pushing hard for Britain joining the Common Market without delay. We need Britain as a broker and to ensure an open door. For if we fail to strengthen our political ties with NATO and don't establish a free world Common Market, we may see the economic community of continental Europe and Africa become a separate political bloc, which could be a third great power, equal in strength to Russia and the United States, and uncommitted between the two. The emergence of such a fortress Europe would crack the historic unity of Western civilization, upon which rest the hopes of free men and free institutions."

could gain some of the advantages of joining the Common Market—opportunities for wider trade at lower tariffs—without joining it and thus paying some of the substantial costs of membership. Britain, it will be remembered, saw real disadvantages in the Common Market if it meant slamming the door on Commonwealth exporters who had hitherto found free entry into the British market, turning its back on its EFTA partners, assuming the major costs of agricultural protectionism in the Common Market, and forfeiting its special relationship with the United States. Thus an important faction within the State Department actually intended to let the Reciprocal Trade Agreements program expire rather than run the risk that an attempt to renew it would relax the pressure on Britain to join the Common Market.

The concentration on the Common Market undoubtedly accounts for the State Department's strange reluctance to prepare a new trade bill, which had to be introduced early in the 1962 session of Congress if the United States were to have new trade authority to replace existing trade legislation when it expired on June 30, 1962. Despite the known expiration date, the State Department did nothing about a trade bill until late in 1961, when Britain's chances of joining the Common Market looked reasonably good. The decision to have a bill at all came from the White House. The bill which went up to the Ways and Means Committee early in 1962 had been so hastily prepared that the committee staff had as its first task the preparation of a 65-page memorandum devoted in large part to technical errors in draftsmanship.

Tailoring the Trade Expansion Act to force Britain in. What was to be the most dramatic single power of the Trade Expansion Act of 1962 was used—or misused—by the State Department during 1962 to attempt to force Britain into the Common Market. The maneuver not only failed, with President de Gaulle's veto of British entry in January, 1963. It also succeeded in eviscerating the act itself.

Here is how it came about. The drafters of the Trade Expansion Act realized that, in order to compel adequate reductions from others, the United States would need power to reduce tariffs by more than a mere 50 per cent. Such a 50 per cent power had been included in several of the trade agreement acts of the Thirties and the Forties. Thus the trade bill contained not only another general authority to cut tariffs 50 per cent, but a new and highly publicized authority to make 100 per cent cuts in negotiations with the Common Market on any commodity of which the United States and the Common Market are together the "dominant supplier"—defined as carrying on at least 80 per cent of the world trade in that commodity.

President Kennedy particularly stressed the tariff-eliminating power in his Jan. 24, 1962, message sending the Trade Expansion Bill to Congress:

> The Trade Agreements Act must be replaced by a wholly new instrument. A new American trade initiative is needed to meet the challenges and opportunities of a rapidly changing world economy.
>
> To be effective in achieving a breakthrough agreement with the EEC so that our farmers, manufacturers, and other Free World trading partners can participate, we will need to use both the dominant-supplier authority (to eliminate tariffs) and the general authority (to reduce tariffs by 50 per cent) in combination.

Secretary of Commerce Luther H. Hodges developed the point further in his testimony for the Trade Expansion Bill before the House Ways and Means Committee on March 12, 1962:

> This 50 per cent authority by itself is simply and clearly not enough to accomplish our objectives concerning the European Common Market. If we were able to reduce our tariffs by no more

than 50 per cent, the EEC could then be expected to impose a similar limitation in its reductions, still leaving an only partially reduced tariff wall as a formidable barrier against many particularly large United States export products.

With the internal tariffs paid by our European competitors being eliminated altogether, this would still leave United States business trying to export to the EEC under a heavy cost disadvantage tariffwise. . . .

The Europeans are moving to free trade; we need authority to go to zero, too, on at least part of our trade which is primarily concerned with European markets. Either we give our exporters a real chance to keep their markets and share in the growth of the new Europe, or we turn our backs in retreat. . . .

The big hitch in the Trade Expansion Act's provision for eliminating tariffs is that it becomes effective only if Britain and several other EFTA countries join the Common Market. If they join, the power to bargain down to zero would apply to some 26 major categories of United States exports, such as automobiles, trucks, and buses; metal working machinery; mining, construction, and other industrial machinery; chemicals; office machinery; power generating machinery; electrical machinery; rubber manufactures; and paper and paper products. But without their joining, the zero bargaining power becomes practically meaningless: the only commodities in which the present Six of the Common Market and the United States account for 80 per cent of world trade are aircraft and margarine!

Senator Paul Douglas of Illinois and I were not inclined to entrust our trading future to Britain's chances of entry. We proposed an amendment to the trade bill which would have given the United States down-to-zero bargaining power on the 26 major groups of commodities, whether or not Britain and the rest joined the Common Market. At the Senate Finance Committee hearing on the proposed amendment on Aug. 16, 1962 (p. 2261) Undersecretary of State George Ball let the cat out of the bag in the course of arguing for the State Department's version of the "dominant supplier" clause, and against the Douglas-Reuss amendment. If the amendment were adopted, he suggested:

We would be injecting ourselves into the UK-EEC negotiations. . . . Opponents of the entry of Britain into the Common Market could say that there was an alternative presented to Britain which had not been available before. They would say the United States had given up hope that Great Britain was going to enter the Common Market and therefore that it was a hopeless enterprise, and so on.

I think that this politically would be a highly undesirable action for the United States to take.

To this Senator Douglas replied: "I would say you have already been injecting yourself on the side of putting pressure on Great Britain to get into the Common Market."

Despite the State Department's argument, the Senate adopted the Douglas-Reuss amendment. But the amendment was removed in conference between the House and the Senate, largely because of House Ways and Means Committee Chairman Wilbur Mills' wish to avoid altering the bill as passed by the House.*

The State Department's activities in the matter of the "dominant supplier" clause were summarized by Robert D. Novak, writing in *The Wall Street Journal:*

This cautious approach tends to confirm suspicions that the provision, ingeniously fashioned in its original form to be effective only if Great Britain joins the Common Market, was intended by the State Department to serve primarily as a shotgun to force a British-European economic marriage. (Actually, the possibility that so historic a step as closer British ties with the Continent would be greatly enhanced by the prospect of lower U.S. tariffs is scoffed at by Europeans.)

* Stanley Metzger, "The Trade Expansion Act of 1962," *Georgetown Law Review,* Spring, 1963.

Thus, because of the State Department's attempt to use the Trade Expansion Act as a counter in the power politics of the Common Market, we made the main provision of the Act "all sound and fury, signifying nothing." And Britain failed to get into the Common Market.

What the Common Market will cost

To count the costs of the Common Market is not to overlook the great benefits to the free world of the Common Market movement. Economically it is giving the Six the same kind of vast internal market that has been the economic foundation of the United States. Politically it has reduced the historic tensions between Germany and France, and helped to pull West Germany into the family of the West.

But Western Europe could have been given the spark of economic competition and of a large free market, and the benefits of Franco-German *rapprochement, w*ithout setting up the particularistic and discriminatory enclave that the Six threatens to be. The Common Market—and EFTA, too, for that matter—could have been allowed to proceed with its internal free trade policy and thus depart from the free worldwide GATT policy of nondiscrimination, in return for its commitment to grant within several years a substantial unilateral tariff reduction to the rest of the world to partially offset the discrimination. GATT, as we have seen, asked for and got such a commitment from the Coal and Steel Community when it was set up. What is fair for trade in two commodities—coal and steel—should have been equally fair for trade in all.

But, rather than lamenting what might have been, let us examine the costs of the Common Market to this country. First, the direct costs. If the Common Market persists in its present policy of making itself largely self-sufficient in food, irrespective of cost, this could mean that we would lose our entire exports to the Six of wheat, feed grains, rice, and poultry.

Our exports of these to the Common Market in 1962 totaled $483 million, about 40 per cent of our total agricultural exports to the Common Market. An interim West German increase in duties on poultry alone has already wiped out United States exports worth $48 million in the preceding year.

It is impossible to calculate the losses, or failures to gain, on our exports of industrial goods, because one cannot predict to what extent members of the Six will be able to displace our exports to the area. The Common Market external tariff on an electric kitchen mixer, for example, is 18 per cent. Germany will be able to sell its mixers in France at a zero tariff. Our own exports are bound to be severely displaced.

Other Common Market tariffs for important American export items are likewise distressingly high—automobiles, 22 per cent; special-purpose motor trucks, 20 per cent; radio and TV receivers, 22 per cent; electronic calculating machines, 14 per cent; ball bearings, 18 per cent. If the Trade Adjustment Act conferred the power to eliminate, not just to reduce by 50 per cent, the Common Market's external tariff, we could do some real bargaining on these items in the upcoming 1964 round. But with our tariff-cutting powers limited to 50 per cent, the Common Market's external tariff would still be substantial, and the likelihood that United States exports will be displaced by duty-free competition from within the area of the Six is a very real one.

The indirect costs to us may well exceed the direct.

Some of the United States' best customers—Japan, Latin America, and Canada and other members of the Commonwealth—are in line to experience sharp losses in their present or potential export sales to the Common Market. As their export earnings decline, they will be able to buy less from the rest of the world, including the United States.

The developing countries in Asia and Africa, other than those associated with the Common Market, are also going to suffer discrimination in their exports. To the extent that they

do, and their earnings go down, they may require that much
more foreign economic aid from the United States.

Other countries are likewise going to suffer from the discrimination by the Common Market against their exports.

Such discrimination may be catastrophic for some European countries not in the Common Market. Exports are the
economic lifeblood of Sweden, Switzerland, Austria, and other
members of EFTA. Their economies are closely interwoven
with those of the Six. Their exports account for a much larger
part of their national product than in the United States. In
Switzerland, for example, exports amount to 13.5 per cent of
gross national product, compared with 4 per cent in the United
States.

And a large share of these exports has traditionally gone
to Common Market countries. Denmark's efficient farmers
have earned about half of the nation's export income. A major
market for their products has been West Germany. However,
as the Common Market agricultural policy goes into effect,
Denmark is already beginning to feel the pinch. The Danes
must anticipate the probable loss of $150 million yearly in
export trade.

The Latin American countries, on their part, face special
problems due to the discriminatory preferences the Common
Market gives to the former French and Belgian territories in
Africa. Argentina will be hurt if the Six proceed to eat duty-
free French grain rather than Argentine grain that must pay
the Common Market external tariff. Brazil will be hurt when
the former French African colonies increase their coffee production and export it to the Six duty-free. Ecuador faces the
same problem as cocoa production shifts to former French
Africa. What the United States gives to Latin America through
the Alliance for Progress it can take away by failure to bargain
away the Common Market's discriminatory policies.

Ironically, if President de Gaulle had not vetoed British
entry into the Common Market in January, 1963, the export

problems facing the rest of the world vis-à-vis the enlarged Common Market area would be even more acute than they now are.

Britain, for example, now accords preferential or duty-free treatment to imports from Commonwealth countries. If the Common Market denied these countries the right to sell the equivalent volume of agricultural products and manufactured goods that they had sold prior to Britain's entry, their export earnings would inevitably fall. On the other hand, if Britain succeeded in obtaining special entry privileges for the grain, meat, dairy products, and fruit of Canada, Australia, and New Zealand into the enlarged Common Market, it would have been at the expense of the United States' own agricultural export market.

The developing countries of the free world, except for the favored former French and Belgian territories, would also face a serious problem. Perhaps Britain would have been able to negotiate a preference similar to that enjoyed by former French and Belgian colonies for some of her former African colonies, such as Ghana and Kenya. But if cocoa, coffee, bananas, can be freely imported into the enlarged Common Market from these favored territories, what of others, such as the former British West Indies? And if the tropical food products of the West Indian territories are permitted preferential treatment, what about their growing textile industries? And if West Indian textiles are admitted into the Common Market duty-free, what about Hong Kong and India?

An endless chain of special bilateral arrangements would be necessary to prevent gross injustice to the poorest members of the British Commonwealth—just the kind of trading pattern which GATT was designed to overcome.*

For other countries—Ireland and Spain in Europe; Israel, Turkey, Iran, and the Arab countries in the Middle East; Latin

---

* See James E. Meade, *UK, Commonwealth, and Common Market* (1962), pp. 31–32.

America, and the unaffiliated countries of Asia and Africa—
the withdrawal of Europe into an enlarged Common Market
could mean anything from serious trade dislocation to potential catastrophe.

Israel, for example, has staked her economic future on expanding trade with Europe. Sixty per cent of her exports now
go to Britain and the Six. By selling oranges, her principal
export earner, to Britain at a nondiscriminatory tariff of 10
per cent—that is, the same tariff paid on oranges from any
other country—Israel can compete successfully with other
orange-growing countries. But if Britain joined the Common
Market, Israel would have to pay a tariff of 20 per cent to sell
her oranges in Britain. It would be hard to compete with
oranges from Italy and North Africa, which are members of
the Common Market and thus pay no tariffs.

The road back to multilateralism and free world community

MUST THE COMMON MARKET CONTINUE TO MESMERIZE US?

The 1964 Kennedy–Johnson round of trade negotiations will
determine the fate of world trade for at least a decade. If negotiations are conducted in 1965, the five-year phasing of tariff
reductions required by the Trade Expansion Act would not be
completed until 1970. The upcoming negotiation, therefore,
is the most important in our history.

The French veto of British entry into the Common Market
means that we will be bargaining with a Common Market
of six, not with one of thirteen or more, which would have
been the case had the Common Market absorbed the EFTA
countries.

Nevertheless, our apparent negotiating strategy for the Kennedy–Johnson round still reflects our old fixation on the Common Market as if it were the center of our solar system.

The preliminary skirmishes. The beginnings of the negotiations were not auspicious. Members of the GATT countries met at Geneva in May, 1963, to frame a set of rules governing the future negotiations. Once again, we kept our gaze fixed on the Common Market. And once again, the compromises reached appeared to require that the United States and other free world countries would have to give more to the Common Market than they would receive in exchange.

One of the main points at issue during the five-day meetings was the Common Market's insistence that high United States tariffs be reduced relatively more than lower Common Market tariffs on the same commodities. We strenuously opposed this suggestion at the outset, pointing out that at least reciprocal cuts were necessary if the present balance-of-payments surplus in favor of the Common Market countries were not to be further increased. In the end, we had to compromise. This means that on at least some items, to be determined by a working committee, we may find ourselves having to agree to 50 per cent cuts in our tariffs in exchange for lower cuts or no cuts at all by the Common Market. The best we can hope for is that, by hard bargaining, this new trading disadvantage will be held to a minimum.

We told the Common Market that we would conclude no bargain on industrial products until the Common Market settled on a common policy for wheat, feed grains, meat, poultry, and rice that was acceptable to the major agricultural exporting countries. Since the Common Market had not arrived at a common policy on these commodities before the GATT session, we asked the Six for an interim agreement to maintain the present level of exports of these commodities into the Common Market. We did not secure such an agreement.

It was our declared objective to secure general agreement

that principal exports of developing countries in non-French Africa, Asia, and Latin America would not suffer discrimination by reason of the association of ex-French and ex-Belgian areas of Africa with the Common Market. We failed to get agreement to this principle. The Common Market specifically maintained the need for such discrimination, and there is no assurance that it will not have its way on the matter.

Our apparent strategy: if the common market balks, we quit. Though the Six takes only one-fifth of our exports (some $4 billion a year), we apparently intend to bargain principally with her and allow the success or failure of such negotiation to determine what we do about the other 40-odd nations in GATT, to whom we sell four-fifths of our exports (some $16 billion annually).

More than that, there are indications that the United States intends to bring the Kennedy–Johnson round to an end if the Common Market fails to rid itself of its agricultural protectionism. "Before we engage in far-ranging tariff reductions on industrial products," Special Trade Negotiator Christian A. Herter told the United States Chamber of Commerce on Apr. 29, 1963, "we feel that we must have indications that the Common Market is not adopting a restrictive trade policy on agriculture."

Unfortunately that is precisely what the Common Market has been doing, to the evident distress of American poultry, wheat, and grain farmers, and their representatives in Congress.

Our bargaining strategy appears to be this: We are going to negotiate mainly with the Common Market; and if she won't give on either agricultural or industrial products, we are going to punish ourselves and the rest of the free world by calling off the negotiations.

The reason given for ending the Kennedy–Johnson round in the event the Common Market is intransigent, without attempting to bargain with the rest of the members of GATT, is that tariffs lowered by such bargaining would simply result in the unjust enrichment of the Common Market because she would have to be extended most-favored-nation treatment. According to Brendan M. Jones, writing in *The New York Times* on Apr. 28, 1963:

Should the Common Market be willing to negotiate only a limited number of tariff reductions with this country in the coming discussions an awkward problem would arise. The effect would be to stymie special negotiations with Britain or Japan, for example.

Tariff cuts made to either of these countries would, under "most-favored-nation" policy, have to be extended to the Common Market. Thus, the Common Market would gain the benefit of an extra tariff concession without making a compensating one of its own to this country.

Such unrequited benefits to the Common Market would go very much against the grain for the United States, especially after limited bargaining by the European bloc. It is probable they would also limit new agreements with other countries.

Consequently, the negotiations with the Common Market are being approached by Administration officials as the key to a general lowering of world trade barriers.

What makes such a bargaining position a strategy headed for almost certain failure is that the conditions of failure—Common Market intransigence—are highly likely to come to pass. True, a number of members of the Six undoubtedly want to be reasonable about the upcoming negotiations. But until weighted voting modifies the veto in 1966, any one member can transform the Six into an unreasonable roadblock. France proved that by its January 14 veto of Britain's entry. The blunt fact is that strong elements exist in the Common Market which are quite content with its proposed agricultural protectionism.

Strong elements exist also which find its relatively high external tariff on industrial goods, coupled with the increasingly free exchange of goods between members of the Six, an economic advantage beyond compare. Here are the mightiest industrial countries of the Continent, invited to form a bloc which gives them a tremendous internal market, and the right to discriminate in their tariffs against the rest of the world— all with the cheers of the free world ringing in their ears! Who wouldn't be happy at being granted a special license to discriminate, while at the same time receiving the applause of those discriminated against?

So the likelihood of intransigence by the Six is very real. A discerning article in *The Economist* for April 13, 1963, discusses the French attitude toward tariff reductions:

Not only would a massive incursion of American goods menace several French industries; too radical a reduction in the common external tariff of the Six would jeopardise the cohesion of the common market. Paris has not gone to so much trouble to exclude Britain only to let in the United States by the back door. Wholesale concessions to the United States would also be detrimental to the agricultural policy of the Six, as well as to their relations with Africa; this, in the eyes of Paris, weighs as heavily as the threat to France's metallurgical, chemical, coal and textile industries.

French industrialists go even further than the Government and . . . in their view a straight-forward application of the same rules to the enormous American trusts and to even the largest European undertakings resembles a struggle between a mouse and an elephant (*pot de terre contre pot de fer*) . . . "How can there be real competition with General Motors," M. Villiers, president of the French employers, recently asked, "so long as its enormous powers, its fabulous capital resources, its considerable profits, enable it to have recourse to a range of marketing and publicity techniques unattainable in Europe?" According to the industrialists, true equality would therefore demand concessions from the United States double or treble those required of Europe.

All this is a gloomy prospect. If the Common Market says "Stop the world, we want to get off!" we are apparently about to punish ourselves and the rest of the free world by calling off negotiations then and there.

A SENSIBLE STRATEGY FOR THE KENNEDY— JOHNSON ROUND: BACK TO MULTILATERALISM

This need not be, provided we sidetrack our present strategy of letting the Common Market call the tune, and instead adopt a strategy directed at the whole free world.

Specifically, we should invite the Common Market to join us at the negotiations in working for restrictions on agricultural and industrial products that are low, low, low, and that are nondiscriminatory throughout the free world.

We should thus make clear to the Common Market right at the start that our aim is free world-wide tariff bargaining, and that we hope that the Common Market will join with us toward that end. Passage, even now, of the Douglas-Reuss amendment to the Trade Expansion Act so as to permit down-to-zero bargaining on a substantial list of commodities would give us some needed elbow-room in negotiating. The present 50 per cent limits on bargaining unnecessarily tie our hands.

But while we work for the best, we must prepare for the worst. If the Common Market should stick to its proposed protective policy on wheat, feed grains, rice, meat, and poultry; or if it refuses to make adequate concessions to the United States, Canada, Australia, New Zealand, Denmark, and the other countries hurt by its farm policy; or if it refuses to bargain in good faith for substantial lowering of tariffs on industrial products—if any of these happens either now or later, we should keep always in mind the legal remedies available to us:

Possible action against protectionism on agricultural products. Suppose the Common Market turns out to be unyielding in its protectionist policy on wheat, feed grains, meat, rice, and poultry. If it is, most United States exports of these commodities, which came to $483 million in fiscal 1962, would be cut off. In such a situation, we have two remedies.

On an unilateral basis, we could invoke Section 252 of the Trade Expansion Act of 1962: "Whenever unjustifiable foreign import restrictions . . . oppress the commerce of the United States . . . the President shall take all appropriate and feasible steps within his power to eliminate such restrictions." Included within the "steps" which the President may take are to "suspend, withdraw, or prevent the application of benefits of trade agreement concessions to products" of the country imposing the unjustifiable restriction.

On a multilateral basis, we could take advantage of Article XXIII of the General Agreement on Tariffs and Trade, which protects countries against the impairment of benefits accruing to them under that agreement by compelling equivalent concessions on other products.

It is hardly likely that the Common Market can offer the United States adequate compensation for agricultural restrictions through reductions of her tariffs on industrial goods. It is impossible for the Common Market to make adequate compensation to countries like Canada, Australia, New Zealand, Argentina, and Denmark, since their exports of industrial goods to the Common Market are insignificant compared to their exports of agricultural products.

Accordingly, if the Common Market adopts its announced agricultural policy, it would be violating Article XXIII of GATT and "nullifying and impairing" concessions previously made by its member countries. Under Article XXIII, a country which is injured by the Common Market's agricultural policy could be authorized to withdraw previous concessions to the Market's member countries and could also be released from any obligation to them.

There is a precedent for such retaliatory action under GATT. In 1951, the United States introduced restrictions on imports of dairy products. Denmark and the Netherlands complained that this action impaired concessions previously granted. As compensation for damage to cheese exports, the

Netherlands government asked the members of GATT to permit it to restrict imports of wheat flour from the United States during 1953. The GATT signatories agreed, allowing the Netherlands to cut its wheat-flour imports from the United States in 1953 from 72,000 to 60,000 metric tons. Congress thereupon allowed the "cheese amendment," which had caused the trouble in the first place, to expire.

More recently, we ourselves had occasion to apply to GATT under Article XXIII. In November, 1962, we informed GATT that France, by maintaining quota restrictions on the import of fresh and processed fruit and vegetables, was impairing concessions that this country had given during the 1960–61 Dillon round. The members of GATT found against France and we were therefore given permission to work out a withdrawal of concessions to France.

If the Common Market persists in agricultural protectionism, there is nothing illiberal about United States retaliation —either under Section 252 of the Trade Expansion Act or under Article XXIII of GATT. We would be guilty of far greater disservice to the cause of liberal trade if our inaction condoned trade discrimination by six of the most prosperous countries in the world.

Retaliatory action by a country which has itself been subjected to protectionist treatment by another has the support of the father of liberal trade himself, Adam Smith:

The case in which it may sometimes be a matter of deliberation how far it is proper to continue the free importation of certain foreign goods, is, when some foreign nation restrains by high duties or prohibitions the importation of some of our manufactures into their country. Revenge in this case naturally dictates retaliation, and that we should impose the like duties and prohibitions upon the importation of some or all of their manufactures into ours. Nations accordingly seldom fail to retaliate in this manner. . . .

There may be good policy in retaliations of this kind, when there is a probability that they will procure the repeal of the high duties or prohibitions complained of. The recovery of a great foreign market will generally more than compensate the transitory inconveniency of paying dearer during a short time for some sorts of goods. To judge whether such retaliations are likely to produce such an effect, does not, perhaps, belong so much to the science of a legislator, whose deliberations ought to be governed by general principles which are always the same, as to the skill of that insidious and crafty animal, vulgarly called a statesman or politician, whose councils are directed by the momentary fluctuations of affairs.*

Possible action against protectionism on industrial products. If the Common Market proves unyielding in its agricultural protectionism, or fails to make adequate compensation for it, or fails seriously to bargain down industrial tariffs, we should not sulk and retire from the negotiating table.

Instead we should vigorously bargain with the United Kingdom, Sweden, Denmark, Norway, Austria, Switzerland, and Portugal—the European Free Trade Association—with Canada, New Zealand, Australia, Japan, and the rest of the members of GATT. It is particularly important that we bargain with the EFTA countries, since by the end of 1966 these countries will have eliminated all tariffs between themselves on industrial products. This discrimination could seriously harm our exports of such products as paper, machinery, vehicles, instruments, and consumer durables. The only way to eliminate the discrimination is to bargain down tariffs of the individual EFTA countries.

Certainly we should not be deterred from vigorous bargaining with all GATT members except an intransigent Common Market by the notion that the benefits of such negotiations would have to be passed on to the Common Market through the most-favored-nation clause contained in Article I of GATT. This is absurd. Trade negotiations are not required

* Adam Smith, *An Inquiry into the Nature and Causes of the Wealth of Nations* (George Routledge & Sons, Limited, London), pp. 354–356.

to give the dog in the manger the biggest bone. Such a conclusion is required neither by the American history of the most-favored-nation clause, nor by the spirit of GATT itself.

The unconditional most-favored-nation principle was first announced for the United States by Secretary of State Charles Evans Hughes back in 1923. Its purpose was and is an entirely valid one: to protect us and the rest of the free world against special deals whereby the party which has just given a trade concession wipes it out by giving somebody else a still more favorable concession.

In the past we have several times discontinued most-favored-nation treatment to countries which discriminated against us. In 1939, for example, we found that Nazi Germany was discriminating against our commerce by the use of various export subsidy devices. We therefore increased tariffs on imports from Germany without also increasing them on the same commodities from other countries. Similarly, we have long refused most-favored-nation treatment to Communist-bloc countries.

If the Common Market, accordingly, does not comply with the reciprocal spirit of the upcoming GATT negotiations to the same extent as do other countries, the following alternatives could be used to prevent the automatic extension of new benefits to the Common Market:

(1) *Amending the most-favored-nation clause.* Article I of GATT, which now provides for general unconditional most-favored-nation treatment for all contracting parties, could be amended so that such treatment shall not be accorded to any country or group of countries which are important suppliers of a product and which refuse to lower tariffs to the equivalent extent as the dominant supplier of the product.* Under the

* This position—that the benefits of tariff reductions should be accorded only to countries willing to give reciprocal reductions—was pressed by the U.S. delegation to the international trade conference at Havana in 1947. See Clair Wilcox, *A Charter for World Trade* (1949), pp. 161–164.

provisions of GATT, such an amendment would require unanimous approval of the membership. If any country chooses to exercise its veto power over amending Article I, other alternatives are available.

For example, interested countries could participate in drafting a new trade instrument—very much like GATT except that it would qualify the most-favored-nation clause. This instrument could then be the basis for new trade negotiations.

Such a new method to cope with emerging trade problems has its most famous precedent in United Nations history. When the power of the Soviet veto threatened paralysis in the Security Council at the time of the Korean crisis in 1950, the United States initiated the "Uniting-for-Peace" procedure in the General Assembly where a veto could not block action. Similarly, if the threat of veto in GATT of an appropriate amendment of Article I prevents the United States and other countries from entering into trade negotiations, we should unite with other countries to make negotiations possible.

(2) *Forming a larger free trade area.* We might, under the provisions of Article XXIV, join with all GATT members other than the Six to form a free trade area under which participating countries would agree to percentage cuts in their entire tariff structure and would work out plans for additional percentage reductions in the future. The benefits of the tariff cuts would not have to be extended to the Six—or to any other country— which refused to go along. It is worth noting that on Jan. 1, 1966, France—most intransigent of the Six—loses her veto power, and can be outvoted on a trade question by the other Common Market members, who might not like being isolated from the rest of the free world.

The door would be open to such countries to enter the free world free trade area whenever they desired. While it is true that under Article XXIV, a free trade area must eliminate tariffs on substantially all of the trade of its constituent territories, it is not required to do this at once. For example, GATT has not disapproved of the European Free Trade Association because it has not begun to reduce agricultural tariffs within the area, nor agreed on a specific plan for such reductions. The wider free trade area, including most of the major trading countries of the free world, would have actual free trade on all commodities only as a remote objective.

Such a free world-wide bargaining strategy in trade fits in with the concept of free world community. In fact, it is likely to produce a more reasonable bargaining attitude by the Common Market than does our present strategy, which merely rewards the Common Market for her obduracy.

Other trade problems. The Kennedy round affords an opportunity to discuss and act upon much besides tariff reductions. Agreements by the free world's industrial countries to increase their imports of industrial products from the developing countries is of prime importance. Elimination of barriers to imports of tropical agricultural products, whether in the nature of a tariff or of an excise tax as in some of the continental countries, should have high priority.

It is also time that the agricultural producing nations start talking about the fundamentals of their domestic farm programs. There must be some limit to the growing of sugar in cold countries at vastly higher cost than it takes to grow it in hot. And is it rational for mountainous Japan to raise beef cattle when the Argentine pampas lie ready?

Nontariff barriers to trade—the Buy American Act; quotas on oil, lead and zinc, and agricultural products in the U.S.; and restrictions abroad, such as German quotas on coal and leather, various export subsidies, and domestic automobile taxes which in effect discriminate against American automobile exports—also require attention.

Another look needs to be taken, too, at East-West trade. Materials with a war potential should continue on our embargo list. But our present policy of forbidding export to the Soviet bloc of goods that merely increase economic well-being can stand reexamination. For one thing, most of our European friends and allies disregard the embargo. When we forbid the export of American steel back of the Iron Curtain, West European steelmen get out their order books and make the sale. The net result: the Communists get the steel, and we lose the jobs and the boost to our balance of payments. But over and beyond this, we may ask whether our strategy is to make the Soviet bloc desperate through want, or more relaxed through prosperity. Upon this hangs future judgment concerning East-West trade.

CHAPTER THREE

An Improved Monetary Mechanism for the Free World

> In the Federal Reserve Act we instituted a great and vital banking system not merely to correct and cure periodical financial debauches, not simply indeed to aid the banking community alone but to give vision and scope and security to commerce and amplify the opportunities as well as to increase the capabilities of our industrial life at home and among foreign nations.
>
> Carter Glass,
> *An Adventure in Constructive Finance*

Emerson once said that he would never understand economics until a poet came along who could make the subject sing. The average American feels much the same way when he is asked to think about the balance-of-payments problem. Indeed I would guess that until recent years he had either never heard the phrase at all or thought that it was some sort of thing that only foreigners had. But then, suddenly, toward the end of the Eisenhower Administration, he heard that the thing—whatever it was—had leaped the Atlantic Ocean and hit the United States hard. It all seemed so strange—if not downright un-American—that the average American was inclined to say: "It's just too complicated for me to understand, much less to share in framing a solution to it."

Regrettably, I am not the Emersonian poet who can make the whole of this subject sing, and so explain it all. But the task of understanding the balance-of-payments problem—and what can be done about it—is far from hopeless. A good place to begin is to visit, as I recently did, the Federal Reserve Bank of New York at Liberty and Nassau streets in the heart of the financial district. Here, in the bottommost vaults 85 feet below the street, I saw row on row of gold bars. Each bar weighed 27 pounds. Each was worth about $14,000. Altogether they had a value of around $13 billion dollars. The gold is all owned by foreign countries, most of it acquired from the United States in the last ten years. Each country's gold is kept in a separate sealed compartment, with security arrangements that could frustrate the acquisitive instincts of any real-life "Lavender Hill Mob." A 90-ton steel vault door glides shut every night, while a force of expert marksmen, constantly on guard, can seal off all escape avenues from the Bank in a matter of seconds.

The Federal Reserve, with its foreign-held gold, dramatizes our recurring balance-of-payments problem and our international financial plight. What's to be done about it? The very place where the question is asked suggests an answer. It is that if the Federal Reserve principle, formulated in response to America's internal needs in a bygone day, were now enlarged along "federal-international" lines, we could turn the whole of our present case for the better.

Here, indeed, is an area in which America, with its long experience in federalism, could lead the way toward an improved monetary mechanism to benefit not only itself but the whole free world. We would do well to recall that before the creation of the Federal Reserve System in 1913, monetary crisis after monetary crisis rocked the United States. Individual banks, communities, and regions of the country lacked the financial reserves required by trade, commerce, and the agricultural cycle from the sowing of seeds to the marketing of crops. Though the United States had filled out the continent and had become a world power, it lacked a nationwide system of payments.

Such elasticity as we had in the supply of money and credit was based primarily on an arrangement that went something like this. In the spring of each year, the great private banks of New York would import capital from the great private banks of Europe, and then reloan that capital to interior banks of the United States, who in turn reloaned it to banks which serviced the American farmer. Then, when the American farmer, who had thus been carried through the sowing and harvesting season, marketed his crops, he would repay his loans to the local banks (beginning in the South and working northward with the sun), and the local banks would repay the interior banks, who in turn repaid the New York banks—and so on back to the European banks. A credit failure in one place could set off a chain of adverse reactions that could spell ruin across the entire nation.

The Federal Reserve of Carter Glass and Woodrow Wilson settled upon a bold innovation. The Federal Reserve was empowered to create bank reserves, and thus an elastic supply of money and credit, and to set up a nationwide method for settling payments between regions of the country. While the system is not perfect, I have heard no one suggest that we should go back to the chaos which prevailed before 1913.

Today the economies of the major free world nations are becoming as interdependent as the economies of the several states were in 1913. When the farmers of West Germany determine to raise more chickens, the broiler growers of Arkansas and Virginia protest. When British interest rates go up, the United States financial authorities know that American funds will take off for London. If the United States cuts its aid program to India, American farms and factories lose sales.

Yet just as the United States lacked a stable system of monetary reserves and of interregional payments prior to 1913, the free world lacks a stable system of reserves and payments today. Unless it wants to stagger from crisis to crisis, the free world must somehow solve the problem of international money.

The thesis of this chapter is that the free world needs something like the basic principle of our own Federal Reserve Act of 1913 "to furnish an elastic currency" which can protect the dollar and other major currencies, and insure the free world enough reserves to permit the expansion of trade and capital investment.

In developing this thesis, we shall see how the decade of deficits in our international payments has shaken our economic might. We shall explore some ways by which we may bring our deficits under control, and stress the necessity of achieving balance promptly. We shall then observe that the money troubles of ourselves and the rest of the free world go deeper than U.S. deficits, and that an improved monetary mechanism for the entire free world is required to set them right. Finally, we shall examine some methods of bringing such a mechanism into being.

Our payments deficit: too much of a good thing

HOW OUR DEFICITS GREW

At the end of World War II, the United States held 60 per cent of the free world's gold reserves, some $24 billion. We also had a virtual monopoly of the capacity to produce industrial goods. When other countries ran short of money, which was almost immediately, we might have stopped shipping them food and industrial goods. Had Uncle Sam wished to become the richest man in the graveyard, he could unquestionably have wound up with all the gold.

Instead, by the Marshall Plan and similar programs, we helped Western Europe and Japan—victor and vanquished alike—back to their feet. Our objective was to build free world strength by transferring dollars, both for immediate use and for reconstituting monetary reserves. And so the dollar became "as good as gold," and we woke up to find ourselves the free world's banker.

Up to a point somewhere in the mid-1950's, this was a good thing. But as the decade rolled along, our continuing deficits and the shift in our reserve position became too much of a good thing. Although we managed to run a comfortable surplus of exports over imports in most years, our big payment items of private investment and military and economic aid expenditures abroad have resulted in large deficits in recent years.

For the six years 1958–63, the total United States deficit in international payments has been $19 billion—an annual average of more than $3 billion.

We settled this by paying out to foreigners over $7 billion in gold, and adding almost $12 billion to our liquid liabilities to them. By the end of 1963, our gold reserve, $23 billion in 1957, had shrunk to something over $15 billion. Our liquid obligations to foreign central banks, treasuries, and the International Monetary Fund came to $16.5 billion, all convertible to gold on demand. In addition, foreign private banks and holders hold another $10.6 billion in bank deposits and other liquid obligations. These could also become claims against our gold supply if they were turned in to central banks for other currencies.

Here are some reasons why we have lost more gold and accumulated more dollar liabilities abroad than we should have liked:

By the mid-Fifties, most major countries had rehabilitated their industries and regained their share of world export markets. But in many cases they continued to discriminate by quotas and other arrangements against United States exports, thus causing us to sell less than we could have.

The formation of the European preferential trading areas of the Common Market in 1958 and the European Free Trade Association in 1959 has had both direct and indirect negative effects on our balance of payments. A direct effect, because even before discriminatory quotas on dollar goods were completely removed, United States exports began to face tariff discrimination in these areas. An indirect effect, because the prospect of large free trade areas (and the additional protection of a substantial tariff wall around the Common Market) caused a substantial outflow of American capital into Europe, which also increased our deficit. Another cause of our capital outflow was the action in 1958 by most of the major countries to make their currencies convertible for current transactions by nonresidents. This made it feasible for U.S. private capital to go into the newly prosperous countries, particularly those in Western Europe, because now they could be sure of getting their money out. In the past three years, United States private investment in Western Europe plus Canada has averaged about $2 billion annually. But meanwhile, most of these countries still retain controls on exports of their own capital. This, plus our slower growth rate, has kept down capital flows in our direction.

Moreover, a major portion of the mutual defense burden has fallen on this country. Despite recently increased purchases by other countries of military equipment in the United States, we still have an annual net payments outflow of over $2 billion for military expenditures alone. Of this amount, $380 million goes to the Common Market countries. This includes what our troops and their dependents spend abroad, plus what we have to pay for local supplies and renting the real estate upon which our troops operate.

We have also maintained a high level of foreign economic

aid, and not until recently have we tried to confine most of this aid to the export of our own goods. Even after this effort, dollar outflow due to aid exceeded $1 billion in 1962. We have had very little offsetting benefit from the aid programs of other countries. They continue to "tie" most of their aid so that purchases must be made there rather than in the United States.

EFFORTS TO STEM THE OUTFLOW

Since 1959, both the Eisenhower and the Kennedy administrations have attempted to improve the United States payments position and thus to minimize our outflow of gold.

The principal means used has been a form of protectionism, even though it is not as blatant as if we had attempted general increases in our tariffs. To the maximum possible extent, the Administration has tied economic and military aid to purchases of American goods, and diverted the procurement of military supplies to American sources. This can result in a very substantial amount of protection: the Department of Defense directive, for example, requires the diversion of defense procurement to the United States from abroad even though the cost is as much as 50 per cent higher than off-shore procurement. According to Prof. Wilson E. Schmidt of George Washington University:

> The invisible tariff employed by the Department of Defense on overseas purchases of equipment, supplies, and materials offsets, in terms of its effect on the average level of United States tariffs, more than one-fourth of the tariff-cutting authority granted to the President [in the Trade Expansion Act of 1962].*

These tying operations may be necessary, but the best that can be said of them is that they are a necessary evil required by balance-of-payments constraints. They greatly increase the cost of our foreign aid programs to the taxpayer. They shelter

* *The Rescue of the Dollar* (1963), pp. 47–49.

high-cost United States industries from foreign competition. They diminish the benefits to the country we are trying to aid by requiring it to spend its aid allocation on higher-priced goods.

Tying arouses resentment in the country whose aid is being tied. Nigeria's Minister of Finance Festus Sam Okotie-Eboh, in his 1960 budget speech, had this to say:

. . . I cannot refrain from expressing my keen disappointment at the change of policy of the United States Development Loan Fund when, towards the end of last year, it was decided that, except in exceptional circumstances, loans could only be made on the basis of their being tied to United States exports. I think the House will appreciate that under a condition of this sort it becomes very difficult for the Government to decide the extent to which it can take advantage of such offers, particularly if it means that Nigeria cannot obtain the goods she needs in the cheapest available market. It is also quite illogical for countries which express a belief in the wisdom of multilateral systems of trade and payments to tie capital exports in a way that is a complete negation of a declared multilateral policy. We in Nigeria I believe have shown by our actions that we are prepared to pursue liberal multilateral policies in our international trade. We look to other countries for them to reciprocate.*

Other methods have also been used to reduce the United States deficit in payments. To cut down on our imports, the amount of duty-free purchases which United States tourists abroad can take home with them has been reduced from $500 to $100. To discourage the outflow of private United States long-term investment capital, tax incentives for United States investments in industrial countries have been reduced. To encourage foreign tourists to visit the United States, a United States Travel Service has been set up in the Department of Commerce. To encourage American exports, credit terms granted by the Export-Import Bank and insurance coverage

* Quoted in *ibid.,* p. 79.

have been broadened. The Department of Commerce supplies additional know-how to American exporters. To encourage foreign central banks and governments to hold dollars instead of demanding gold, the ceiling on the interest rate that American banks may pay on such accounts has been removed. To reduce the balance of payments costs of our military expenditures abroad, we persuaded the German and Italian governments to purchase increasing amounts of military hardware in the United States.

Our position today would unquestionably be worse in the absence of these measures. But the measures are obviously not enough. The years of $3 billion deficits, which started in 1958, are still with us.

In the summer of 1963, it became apparent that more needed to be done about our balance of payments. President Kennedy's message of July 18, 1963 outlined some steps to be taken. Taken altogether, the Administration hoped that these measures would cause about $2 billion of our $3-billion-plus deficit to disappear.

Continued emphasis was to be placed on measures for expanding our exports, more tourism in this country, and cutting down on the balance-of-payments impact of our military defense and foreign aid programs. But several new measures were proposed.

The first new measure was an "interest equalization tax" on long-term capital outflows, other than for direct investment.

In 1962, new foreign issues of bonds and stock floated in Wall Street totaled $1.2 billion. For the first half of 1963, they were running at a rate of well over $1.5 billion. While a portion of these issues was bought by foreigners, most were bought by Americans, and thus represented a very substantial drain on our balance of payments. The purpose of the "interest equalization tax," ranging from 2.7 per cent to 15 per cent of the value of bonds, and 15 per cent of the value of stocks, is to increase the cost to foreigners of doing their long-term financing in the United States.

All countries of Europe except West Germany restrain foreign access to their own capital markets, and Germany has a law on its books which can be used if capital outflows prove troublesome. For a long time, reputable European financial leaders have been puzzled by our willingness to keep our Wall Street capital market wide open even to countries with a balance-of-payments surplus. Dr. Max Iklé, Managing Director of the Swiss National Bank, said in an Oct. 20, 1962, speech:

> The Swiss monetary authorities have repeatedly pointed out to their American colleagues that, although this willingness to supply the world with capital is very generous and deserves gratitude, such generosity is hard to understand if capital exports endanger the United States balance of payments and its currency. . . . From our point of view, we should prefer equilibrium in the balance of payments and reduced capital exports, because we feel it to be important for confidence in the dollar to be restored as soon as possible.

And a July, 1963, article in the *London Financial Times* pointed out:

> One of the silliest aspects of the international financial scene at the moment is that the continental countries, with far larger external reserves than they know what to do with, are regularly going to the New York capital market for funds to finance their development activities.
>
> They are thereby adding to the stress on the U.S. balance of payments to such an extent that they are having to be asked to put normal dollar convertible arrangements in indefinite suspense, this so that the U.S. can borrow from them on short term the funds it needs to sustain its long-term capital exports to them.

The second element in the Administration's program was to raise the rediscount rate paid by the Federal Reserve from 3 to 3½ per cent—a most dubious move.

Another decision was for the United States to draw up to $500 million in foreign convertible currencies from the International Monetary Fund during the next year. This is the very purpose for which the fund was set up, and our decision to use it to help finance our deficit was long past due.

CUTTING DEFICITS THE WRONG WAY
COULD WORSEN MATTERS

No nation can run deficits in its international balance of payments forever. At some point, international institutions and other countries will no longer be willing to extend credit, and the deficit country will lose all of its reserves. In the case of the United States and Britain, whose currencies are widely held as international reserves, deficits which undermine confidence can start a run on gold. In the process, the free world economy can be disrupted.

So you can find no one to argue that a payments deficit can be continued forever. Everybody in the Administration and in Congress is for ending the deficit. The only question is *how?*

It is first necessary to dispose of some wrong ways of ending our deficit. I shall discuss five commonly heard cure-all proposals:

Devalue the dollar. The monetary system set up by the Bretton Woods Agreements of 1944 consists of more or less fixed, rather than freely fluctuating, exchange rates (exchange rate changes up to 10 per cent may be made by an IMF member unilaterally, greater by IMF agreement). International reserves are today held mainly in gold, dollars and the pound sterling, and in rights to borrow the IMF's currency holdings. Under United States law and the IMF agreement, the price of gold is fixed at $35 an ounce. Thus other currencies are anchored to the dollar, and the dollar is anchored to gold.

Devaluation of the dollar is sometimes urged as a cure for

our balance-of-payments deficit, on the theory that, in terms of foreign currencies, this would enable us to export more and import less. For example, an American devaluation vis-à-vis Germany would mean that the price of American road-building machinery in Germany would go down, and thus our exports increase, and that the price of Volkswagens here would increase, and thus our imports decline.

The Administration has wisely rejected devaluation. For if the United States devalued the dollar, other leading industrial countries would almost inevitably devalue their currencies correspondingly. Thus our deficit would remain the same. But we would actually be worse off than we are now, since foreign holders of dollars, both private and official, having once been burned, would in the future be twice shy about accumulating dollars. The dollar would almost certainly lose its present status as an international currency. Foreigners holding dollars would rush to trade them for other currencies, or for our gold. World monetary reserves would shrink, and trade and financial transactions would be sharply curtailed.

But even if our devaluation were not followed by devaluation of other major currencies, a unilateral United States devaluation could well swing the pendulum too far the other way. We might be trading our deficit for surpluses which could lead to a chain of devaluations by others later on. Meanwhile, the dollar might well have ceased to retain its value as international money.

A general devaluation, with the consent of all major countries, by raising the price of gold is sometimes advocated. True, the immediate effect would be to increase the total of world reserves by the increase in the valuation of the gold. But I doubt that this would be the final result. This extra obeisance to gold, paid by raising its price, might well make individuals more likely to hoard gold, and thus prevent its getting into world reserves. And financial authorities might show a pru-

dent preference for holding a higher ratio of gold in their reserves in the future. So there might well be a loss rather than
a gain in needed world reserves.

In any case, a general devaluation would have extremely
uneven effects. The windfall profits would accrue mainly to
countries like the United States, Great Britain, Switzerland,
or the Netherlands, which traditionally maintain a high proportion of gold in their international reserves, rather than to
countries like Japan, Canada, and Western Germany, which
hold a large percentage of their reserves in dollars. Ironically,
the leading gainers would be the Soviet Union and South
Africa, the two largest gold producers—neither of which is
currently thought to be an appropriate object of our bounty.

As an alternative to devaluation, a system of flexible exchange rates is sometimes advocated. This would involve a
junking of the principle of fixed exchange rates which is the
basis of the International Monetary Fund. More importantly,
it would introduce uncertainty in international trade and investment, which goes directly counter to the need for expanding both. If you wish to sell goods or invest capital in a foreign
country, you want assurance that the price of your sale, or the
value of your investment, is not going to be jeopardized by
a fluctuation against you of the exchange rate. Private hedg-
ing and official stabilization operations could be very costly,
and insufficient to remove the risks.

Proponents of flexible exchange rates argue that modest
shifts in rates tend to have a wholesome "equilibrating" effect on a country's balance of payments—for example, the
decrease in the value of a deficit country's currency tends to increase exports and cut down on imports, thus producing balance. But experience with flexible exchange rates shows that
speculative pressures and psychological factors often result
in cumulative movements which are "destabilizing" rather
than "equilibrating." Fluctuation in the French franc during

1919–26, of the pound sterling in 1921, and the United States dollar in 1933, under systems of flexible exchange rates, brought on severe international monetary troubles.

The more or less fixed exchange-rate system of Bretton Woods has survived for almost two decades. With the free world moving toward expanded trade, fixed exchange rates are at least one vestige of the past worth preserving—provided there is an adequate international monetary mechanism to give countries elbow room to avoid recessions.

Stop our foreign aid program. We have already "tied" our foreign aid program so that almost 80 per cent of its expenditures are made in the United States. To make further cuts in the program for balance-of-payments reasons would be to depart from our national objective that the duty of rich nations is to help poor nations to help themselves. The program should be continued despite frequent exasperation. I recall at a recent monetary conference being buttonholed by the finance minister of a developing country, who lectured me sternly on the need for the United States to put its balance of payments in order. The subject was quickly changed when I pointed out how enormously we could help our payments deficit by cutting down our foreign aid program.

Jettison our military commitments. It may well be that future changes in our military disposition will enable us to reduce our present net outflow of around $2 billion a year for military defense abroad. In Europe, for example, we may find that some number less than the present 360,000 United States servicemen will do the job of convincing the Russians, and our Western European allies, that we consider an attack on Western Europe an attack on ourselves. De Gaulle has as much as said that the number of American troops in Germany could be substantially reduced without weakening the American contribution to Europe's defense—which he thinks is pretty weak, anyway. A British Labour government, if one takes office, believes that American troops can be reduced. While the very mention of troop reduction has caused cries of anguish in Bonn in the past, Chancellor Adenauer's successors may well wonder whether so large an American presence as we now have in Germany is worth the cost to the United States balance-of-payments deficit, or the possibility that the Federal Republic will have to pick up a larger share of the total cost in the future.

All of this can well mean fewer American troops in Europe two years from now than today, with no disruption to the alliance. If it were accompanied by some sort of thinning out of Russian and satellite troops in central Europe, whether as a part of a formal "disengagement" or not, so much the better.

Reduce imports.　Our commitment to liberalize trade is too important to sacrifice on the altar of balance-of-payments constraints. While trade restrictions might in the short run reduce our payments abroad, our advantage would disappear as other countries, with their earnings from us reduced, had to curtail their purchases from us. And the free world at large would lose as less efficient producers took over the markets of the more efficient.

Raise interest rates.　Never has a government tortured itself more than has the United States government over the question of raising interest rates as a means of improving our balance of payments. From the domestic standpoint, tighter credit, and consequent higher interest rates, are valid prescriptions for the economy only when it is at or approaching full employment, and the economy must be dampened if inflation is to be avoided. But the American economy has for years had an unemployment rate of close to 6 per cent, and a capacity to produce each year some $30–$60 billion more goods and services than the amount we have actually produced.

In such a climate, tightened credit and higher interest rates are precisely what the economy does not need.

With respect to short-term credit, tightened credit and higher interest rates particularly hurt small business—often the most inventive and productive—because it relies very largely on bank credit. Because short-term credit is used for carrying inventories, increases in short-term interest rates are a tax on business generally, usually passed on to the consumer. And the enormous amount of consumer credit for installment plan purchases of everything from a new refrigerator to a summer vacation trip depends very largely on bank credit. So increases in the availability and cost of short-term credit hamper both business investment and consumer purchases.

Increases in long-term interest rates have an even more deadening effect upon the economy. They raise the cost of the bond issues by which schools and hospitals and other local improvements are built, and frequently discourage building them altogether. They raise the cost of business investment across the board, and thus discourage the very increases in productivity which are the best way of eliminating balance-of-payments deficits. They raise the cost of home mortgages and deter building generally.

These are the reasons why tight money and higher interest rates go counter to economic growth and full employment at home.

The argument for higher interest rates is that if interest were higher, more people, both Americans and foreigners, would make and maintain their investments in the United States instead of seeking higher returns abroad. Since capital outflows, both short- and long-term, have at various times been important items in our balance-of-payments deficits, a plausible case can be made for raising United States interest rates.

Plausible, in my opinion, but misguided. Saving $1 billion or so on capital outflow—assuming that an interest rate increase would do this—is grossly disproportionate to the potential scores of billions in increased gross national product which we jeopardize by willfully trying to raise interest rates. If ever there was a case of the tail wagging the dog, this is it. This, then, is the "conflict" between the domestic and international aspects of high interest rates. How has it been resolved?

It took a while for the proponents of the high-interest-rate panacea to prevail. At first, a genuine effort was made to harmonize the need for full employment and growth at home, and balance-of-payments equilibrium abroad. Thus the decision of the Federal Reserve System late in 1960 to give up its policy of purchasing only short-term Treasury bills in the open market was hailed as a wise resolution. For nine years prior to 1960, the Federal Reserve had been following a doctrinaire policy of buying and selling only very short-term Treasury securities when it wished to vary the amount of bank reserves, and hence the general availability of credit. The Fed's justification was that if it bought longer-term securities—say, twenty-year United States bonds—it would be affecting the long-term investment market rather than the "equivalent of money" market represented by short-term bills. Under the "bills only" policy, short-term Treasury securities bore the whole brunt of the Fed's purchasing practices. Their price tended to go up, and their yield down. With the recognition of our balance-of-payments problem, and the abandonment of the "bills only" policy, a smaller portion of the Fed's purchasing power was turned loose on bills; their prices went down, and their yields rose. Foreign short-terms lost some of their relative attractiveness over United States Treasury bills.

So far, so good. The "bill" rate in 1961 and 1962 rose about a percentage point, to about 3 per cent. Meanwhile, long-term interest rates held relatively stable. Industrial bond yields, for example, held steady during this period at 4½ per cent.

But then came a prolonged campaign to convince the gov-

ernment of the United States that what was needed was cal-
culated action by the monetary authorities to make interest
rates artificially high—all for balance-of-payments reasons.

After all—so the argument ran—the countries of Western
Europe, in their remarkable recovery of the Fifties, had found
high interest rates no obstacle to full employment. Indeed,
they had accumulated vast surpluses in their international payments during this period. It was therefore an easy matter to
advise the United States that high interest rates was a good
remedy here, too. The fact that most of those giving the advice
were from financial backgrounds congenial to high interest
rates did not make their advice more difficult to give.

The European central bankers' central bank—the Bank for
International Settlements at Basle, Switzerland—repeatedly
raised the call for higher short-term rates as a means of check-
ing the United States payments deficit. More recently, in its
June, 1963, report, the Bank stressed the need for such increases in long-term interest rates as well.

This advice was music to the ears of the majority of the
seven-man board of governors of the Federal Reserve Bank.
Chairman William McChesney Martin, Jr., in 1960 was rest-
ing after a five-year battle in which the Fed had used tight
money and higher interest rates as its main weapon against
a nonexistent demand inflation. What price increases there
had been were largely the result of administered wage-price
inflation, to which tight money offered no counterpoise.

But when the advice, foreign and domestic, started pour-
ing in, Chairman Martin reacted like an ancient firehorse who
has once again heard the siren. In December, 1962, and again
in May, 1963, the Fed used balance-of-payments considerations as its reason for tightening money—by slowing the
growth in total reserves and the money supply, and by reducing the amount of "free reserves" in the nation's banking system from $500 million down to approximately $150 million.
And in July, 1963, with Administration approval, the Fed

raised the rediscount rate from 3 per cent, where it had been since 1960, to 3½ per cent.

All this was done at a time when unemployment, far from improving, was growing worse, and when the national growth rate was still lagging.

It is always difficult to determine when a Federal Reserve policy is also the policy of the Executive Branch generally. But on July 8, 1963, in his testimony before the Joint Economic Committee, Treasury Secretary Dillon had this to say:

There is strong evidence that a substantial portion of short-term capital flows are markedly sensitive to interest rate differentials. Because of this fact, and in the light of the size of our continuing over-all balance of payments deficit, we must recognize the possibility that the monetary authorities may at some point feel obliged to take further action designed to influence those rates that are particularly significant for our balance of payments.

Three days later, the Federal Reserve, with Administration approval, raised the rediscount rate.

Such studies as have been undertaken of the occult business of short-term capital movements are, to say the least, contradictory on what effect interest rate differentials have on short-term capital movements. Dr. Philip Bell of Haverford College, in a paper prepared for the Joint Economic Committee, concluded that the effect of interest-rate differentials was relatively small, and that the need for trade balances, speculation, and other causes were much more important. Dr. Peter Kenen of Columbia University, in an October, 1962, study made for the Treasury, was somewhat more impressed by the effect of interest rate differentials, but said:

I am loath to recommend that the United States raise its interest rates to discourage short-term capital movements, even that they be kept at present levels if the domestic situation argues for reductions. My conclusions as to interest sensitivity are not decisive. Even if they were, the costs at home would be excessive.

In the present state of statistical science, I doubt very much that one can prove that interest rate differentials appreciably affect short-term capital flows, or for that matter that they do not. Yet a national policy of higher short-term interest rates rests on such a flimsy foundation. What we do know is this. Tightened short-term credit and higher interest rates hurt employment and growth; in the long run we will thus be less able to compete in world markets; and our balance of payments will worsen, not improve.

Moreover, it is highly likely that short-term interest rate increases will spill over and cause higher long-term interest rates, even though present abundant savings in the United States, looking for domestic investment opportunities, have tended so far to keep long-term interest rates from increasing. Even if one could conclusively establish that modest interest-rate differentials actually had cost us hurtful capital outflows, the remedy still should not be raising our own rate structure.

If the increases in our interest rate structure are only slight, they would do little to stop capital outflow or induce inflow. Many European borrowers would come to New York even if our interest rate structure were somewhat higher. This is true not only because our capital market is more developed, but because European bank lending rates are often much higher than they appear to be because of special taxes and charges. And American capital moves abroad into direct investments or long-term portfolio investments not because of higher interest rates, but in the hope of higher profits.

Even if our interest rate structure were substantially increased, it would not help our balance of payments for long. If we raise our interest rates, many European countries now facing inflation will feel freer to raise their rates, and our advantage could be quickly lost. Besides, higher interest rates could attract little European resident capital, since nearly all European countries prohibit free capital export.

Far better than to raise interest rates for balance-of-payment reasons would be two methods that we have not yet sufficiently tried: urging other industrial nations to *lower* their interest rate structure, by relying increasingly on taxing more and spending less as an anti-inflationary weapon; and endeavoring to secure an adequate international monetary mechanism, as described below, which can remove the sting from any capital outflows we may experience as a result of interest-rate differentials.

Can it really be that an iron law of nature has visited upon us a perpetual tight-money policy, regardless of our domestic needs, simply because capital may now move freely from country to country? I doubt it.

TO END OUR DEFICIT WILL TAKE TIME

I have been speaking so far of the wrong ways to stop our deficits. I turn now to consideration of some of the more promising ways:

Bargain down foreign tariffs and other trade barriers. Provided that American industry continues to be as resourceful as it has in the past, we can only gain by a generally lower level of world tariffs. The tariff-cutting talks to be held in Geneva in 1964 are vital to us, particularly because of the growing discriminations of the Common Market and EFTA against our trade. While some of the compromises on negotiating rules we have had to make with the Common Market are disturbing, hard bargaining can yet open up new markets for American exporters. But we will be doing well to maintain our present $5-billion annual trade surplus of exports over imports.

Press other countries to eliminate capital controls. With ample monetary reserves, countries like France and Italy should permit far greater freedom to resident capital. As in

Germany, such countries should permit listing of new foreign securities on their exchanges, and their citizens should be as free to buy securities in New York as in Paris or Milan. This would help our balance of payments both by increasing capital inflow, and by permitting American businesses in Europe to raise local European capital for expansion. The Ford Motor Company of Germany, for example, was able recently to list 150,000 shares of its stock on the Frankfurt and Duesseldorf exchanges.

Reduce United States long-term private capital outflow to developed countries.   A drastic rise in 1963 in the rate of private long-term investment of United States capital abroad warns us that this payments item has become a major source of our adverse payments balance. From an annual average of less than $1 billion in the years 1950–55, private long-term investment abroad ranged between $2.5 and $3 billion in the years 1956–62 and jumped to an annual rate in excess of $4 billion in the first half of 1963. About half of these funds were spent for newly issued foreign securities in the United States capital market, while most of the remainder went into investment by United States businesses abroad.

The proposed "interest equalization tax" should curtail capital outflow due to the sale of foreign securities in the United States capital market. It will not affect the second growing cause of our payments imbalance—United States direct investment abroad. There are strong grounds for taking action to diminish this swelling outflow into foreign direct investment.

First, as in the case of long-term capital raised by the sale of securities in our capital market, long-term funds for direct investment abroad are going more and more into the developed countries—particularly to prosperous Western Europe—which are well able to finance their own capital needs.

Second, unlike our direct investment in earlier years, which was mainly for developing petroleum and other raw-material resources and which often yielded high dividend returns in a relatively short time, investment in recent years has been increasingly in Western European manufacturing operations. An example is Chrysler's 1963 purchase of the French ownership of Simca. Investment in such manufacturing operations frequently has adverse effects on our balance of payments. Not only are earnings of United States subsidiaries plowed back into further foreign expansion, thus curtailing our receipts of dividend income. Their output can displace United States exports, both in Europe and in third markets, thus reducing our export receipts. Also, to the extent that United States subsidiaries ship goods into the United States, our imports go up.

Third, foreign countries do not always welcome large-scale take-overs of their industrial facilities by American firms. Japan, for example, has always been reluctant to invite this type of investment, and more recently Canada and France have become alarmed at the extent of United States ownership of their manufacturing industries.

Direct investment outflow to developed countries could be curtailed either directly by requiring advance approval of new investment, or by taxing the earnings of new investment, whether or not they are distributed, at a sufficiently high rate. There are advantages and disadvantages in both methods, and careful consideration must be given to find a balance of advantage. Immediately, the President might well issue a public statement that additional United States private investment in the developed countries is not in the public interest. If such moral suasion does not suffice, we should be prepared to institute other measures.

Maintain pressure to keep foreign interest rates low. Through central bank cooperation and the lending of foreign-owned dollars in the Euro-dollar market, European interest rates are being brought down to significantly lower levels. To the extent that interest-rate differentials affect capital movements, it is much better for this country that the gap be closed by lower European rates than by higher American rates.

European countries could materially help the United States if they relied, in their fight on domestic inflation, less on monetary means, such as high interest rates, and more on fiscal means, such as taxing more or spending less. Raising their own interest rates may help fight inflation, but it also tends to suck away United States capital, and thus intensify our balance-of-payments problem.

Press our European allies to increase defense and aid commitments. This shibboleth cannot be repeated too often, but the prospects of getting substantial additional help appear meagre. We should nonetheless continue to point out the glaring inequities of sacrifices. In 1962, for example, our defense costs took 9.8 per cent of our gross national product, compared to only 6.5 per cent in France, 5.1 per cent in West Germany, 3.5 per cent in Italy, 6.4 per cent in Great Britain, and 4.5 per cent in Canada.

Keep United States prices stable. Price stability—the absence of inflation—is an important domestic goal. It is also an important goal of foreign economic policy, since rising United States prices will frustrate any progress we might make in our exports. What is needed, therefore, particularly as we move toward full employment, is to restrain wage and price increases. The Council of Economic Advisers has, since 1962, evolved a set of guidelines for wage-price policy. But there needs to be worked out a better method of applying these criteria to specific cases.

Boost our economic growth rate. A higher growth rate accompanied by price stability is the best road of all to balance-of-payments equilibrium. It will stimulate new investment and increased productivity, which will give our products a competitive edge in world markets. New technology and new products will broaden our export base. While imports will also increase as our national income increases, United States capital will tend to stay at home, and foreign capital will be attracted here.

When is our payments deficit going to be rectified? The Treasury, which had predicted its rectification in 1963, has missed its guess. Prediction is indeed a difficult matter. As Sir Donald MacDougall has said:

I have come to the conclusion that the only thing which can be said with certainty about any country's balance of payments is that it changes when one least expects it, and often in the opposite direction.*

The Brookings Institution study of August, 1963, hopes that the United States payments deficit will be eliminated, or at least reduced to manageable proportions, by 1968. This is on the assumption that we will have attained close to full employment, and enjoyed price stability, while our European allies have had some continuing inflation. The question, of course, is: What do we do if the estimate of 1968 proves incorrect; and what, in any event, do we do in the meantime?

Monetary troubles go deeper than deficits

LACK OF MECHANISM IS THE REAL TROUBLE

All that has been said so far is to the point that large recurring deficits like ours cause trouble. The longer they continue, the less our creditors will be willing to go on accumulating dollars, and the more they will be inclined to demand gold. In fact, our fears about their fears lead us to all sorts of unwisdom. We throttle domestic growth and employment by raising interest rates; we reduce the effectiveness of our military

* *The Dollar Problem* (1960), p. 64.

defense and our foreign aid by cutting it, or "tying" it to American purchases; we are constantly tempted to adopt unwise trade policies for balance-of-payments reasons. So let us eliminate the deficit.

But to keep the dollar sound internationally, it is not enough for the United States to eliminate its payments deficit.

Apart from the $28 billion in public and private foreign claims on our gold supply, Americans with vast liquid resources could send huge amounts of dollars abroad. If unusual speculative opportunities beckoned, this could happen when our own basic payments situation was as solid as a rock.

Secondly, the gold-demanding proclivities of foreign central banks could well become embarrassing. If existing dollar claims shifted from low-gold-ratio countries like Japan, Canada, or Western Germany to high-gold-ratio countries like Britain, Switzerland, or the Netherlands, we could lose more gold even when our dollar liabilities abroad were being reduced.

Thirdly, the end of our balance-of-payments deficit may well bring in its wake action by Western European countries that will hurt us and the free world. As our deficits decline, European surpluses and thus reserves will correspondingly decline. This will tempt the Western European countries to raise barriers against our imports, to restrict their foreign aid and defense contributions, to impose further clogs on capital movements—all actions harmful to us.

Lastly, if the United States deficit is eliminated, dollars which have provided the leading source of growth in free world reserves—more than gold and sterling—will no longer be available. This will put the free world in a real bind for international reserves, and the road to autarchy will be opened.

The real difficulty we are in, therefore, is not so much our current balance-of-payments deficit, but the exposure of the dollar and other free world currencies irrespective of the payments positions of individual countries.

WEAKNESSES OF THE PRESENT INTERNATIONAL
MONETARY MECHANISM

Today's international monetary system is inadequate for the simple reason that reserves are insufficient for probable needs. There are at least four reasons why international reserves need to be larger today than in the past:

Expanded world trade. The greater the volume of world trade, the greater the likelihood of temporary deficits by one country or another, and the larger the reserves needed to finance those deficits.

Shifts in demand and technology. To an unprecedented degree, the economies of the leading trading countries tend to change, particularly because of changes in demand. When consumers started demanding synthetic fibers rather than silk, Japan had to make some adjustments in order to stay alive. When, in the late Fifties, the international airlines shifted from propeller to jet planes, the United States was in a fortunate position in being able to supply jets to the European countries. Conversely, and at about the same time, a shift in American consumer preference to compact cars which caught Detroit napping resulted in European compacts' taking over a considerable share of the American automobile market, until American manufacturers brought out their own compacts.

Sometimes the shift may be in technology, as when Britain after World War II shifted from her dying coal and textile industries to the engineering industries. Or the disequilibrium may be due to a strike, as when the 1959 United States Steel strike opened the door to unprecedented foreign imports.

Whatever the cause of these shifts, frequently they require several years for an adjustment. A large amount of reserves is needed to tide a country over this period.

Defense and aid requirements.   The need for these goes on equally in time of deficit as in time of surplus. To countries like the United States that have accepted these obligations, it can impose a requirement of large reserves.

Hot money flows.   The convertibility of currency since 1958, and the building up of enormous reserves of liquid capital in most of the developed countries, has greatly increased the potential size of short-term capital outflows. And the possibility of devaluations makes speculative movements of short-term capital the more attractive. Holders of capital remember the extensive devaluations of the European currencies in September, 1949, as well as the upward revaluation of the German mark and the Dutch guilder in April, 1961. Ill-founded rumors that the dollar was to be devalued in October, 1960, saw an enormous transfer overseas by Americans of their liquid assets. The potential size of these flows requires much larger reserves today than in the past.

The total supply of free world reserves is made up of monetary gold, holdings of the dollar and sterling, and the amount of credit that countries may get from the International Monetary Fund and, in a pinch, from foreign central banks. Over-all these reserves may perhaps be adequate at the moment, largely because of the substantial amount of dollars held by foreigners in their reserves.

But the "adequacy" of reserves over-all is meaningless, because reserve crises occur in single countries or groups of countries, not throughout the whole world. The United States and many other countries simply lack an adequate supply of reserves for their foreseeable short-term individual needs.

To illustrate this, let's look at the current reserve position of the United States. We have a gold supply of $15 billion plus, and a small amount of convertible currencies, in our monetary reserves.

On the other side of the balance sheet, as of mid-1963, foreign governments and international institutions owned $19.3 billion in liquid dollar assets, and private holders abroad owned another $8.6 billion. And, as we have seen, we have been running a $3-billion-plus payments deficit a year for the last six years, with the end not in sight.

The supplements to our gold and foreign currency reserves consist in certain availabilities under the International Monetary Fund and under bilateral agreements made with a variety of European countries. The trouble with these existing supplements is that they are too small in amount and too uncertain in availability to be anything like a worry-free safeguard for the dollar. Let us look at them:

The International Monetary Fund and the 1962 supplementary credit agreement. The IMF is the major source for supplementing national monetary reserves. It is a *fund* of gold and currencies, not a superbank with credit-creating powers. It can lend only what it has on hand or can itself borrow. Despite the impressive total of $15 billion in IMF subscriptions, more than $6 billion are the subscriptions of the United States and the United Kingdom. Of the remainder, a substantial part represents the quotas of numerous small countries whose currencies are of little help, or of countries also under reserve pressure.

Today, for example, the most the fund could readily provide the United States in hard currencies (other than sterling or Canadian dollars) would be about $1 billion, plus perhaps another $1 billion in gold.

Beyond this point, we could borrow under the terms of the ten-nation supplementary IMF agreement signed in 1962. This agreement provides $6 billion in various currencies on a standby basis. But again the commitments of the United States, Britain, and Canada are more than half of the total. Moreover, access to the $2.8 billion in currencies which might

be of use to the United States is by no means assured. There
is no firm advance commitment to lend, as there is in the case
of fund subscriptions. Each country retains veto power over
its own participation on any loan request.

The IMF's present capacity to lend is simply not large
enough. Suppose, for example, that the annual deficit of $3
billion which we have had for the past six years were to continue, despite every effort on our part, for another five years.
(The deficits would be worse, of course, in the event of a
sudden flight of capital from the United States.) Against a
total United States need for credit of $15 billion, there would
be available—if we are lucky—a maximum one-time supply
of IMF credit of something less than $5 billion. We would
fall short of our needs by $10 billion, and the IMF would have
drastically reduced its ability to provide for the requirements
of other member countries.

The Treasury–Federal Reserve bilateral loan agreements.
The Treasury and the Federal Reserve have recently entered
into agreements to swap currencies with a number of European
central banks. Including the recently concluded $500 million
agreement with the Bank of England, we now have access to
almost $2 billion in foreign currencies. Currencies borrowed
under these agreements are primarily for the purpose of permitting the United States to engage in spot and forward foreign exchange transactions, and thereby to reduce short-term
capital outflows and speculative attacks on the dollar. Although
the agreements have proved extremely useful for this purpose,
they help only for the short term—90 days or so.

The Treasury recognized that the swap agreements alone
could not prevent a serious gold outflow. Beginning in October, 1962, it has therefore sold special nonmarketable securities to Austria, Italy, Switzerland, Belgium, Canada, Sweden,
and Germany, mostly with maturities of fifteen months to two
years. As in the case of the swap agreements, most of these

securities are payable in the other country's currency, so that the lender has a firm exchange value guarantee. While the amount of such securities outstanding in mid-1963 came to the respectable total of $788 million, only $286 million are unconditionally medium-term loans. The remainder are callable on two days' notice for replacement by 90-day nonmarketable certificates.

In view of the dimension of our needs for possible rescue operations, these bilateral techniques are obviously insufficient. The amount of credit available is nowhere near what is needed. Moreover, most of it is uncertain because it can be withdrawn at the end of 90 days.

Quite apart from the current need to protect the dollar against runs, there is the problem of having enough free world reserves in the future as trade expands. The Treasury's apparent program to get an adequate amount of total reserves is to hold other strong currencies as part of our own monetary reserves. In the future, other countries would be encouraged to hold a number of strong currencies in their reserves, not just the dollar and sterling. In keeping with this long-term plan, the Treasury has already accumulated a small stock of German marks, Swiss francs, Italian lire, and other foreign currencies.

The difficulty—and it is a serious one—with such a multiple key currency system is that it would actually increase the instability of the world's monetary system. At any given time, some countries are sure to be in deficit, and their currencies would tend to be dumped by countries holding them.

Creating an adequate international monetary mechanism

An adequate international monetary mechanism must enable any major industrial country in payments difficulties to finance itself promptly, in adequate amounts, and for a long enough time so that constructive policies can restore equilibrium. Immediately, the United States appears to be the principal beneficiary of such an improved mechanism. But as United States deficits come to an end, and other countries thus lose an important source of reserves, an alternative source of reserves under such an improved mechanism is equally necessary for them.

Gold production is clearly going to be insufficient as a means of providing adequate future world reserves. In 1962, for example, free world gold production was $1.5 billion, but only $305 million of it wound up in its monetary reserves. The rest of the free world's need for reserves was met by foreign monetary authorities' adding about $1 billion in dollars to their reserves. The existing sources of reserves—gold, dollars, and sterling—are obviously completely haphazard.

Dozens of plans have been suggested, ranging all the way from going back to the old gold standard to creating a world superbank. Edward M. Bernstein of Washington, Prof. Robert Triffin of Yale, and others are leading exponents of various plans. The broad terms of what an acceptable plan should contain were set forth in a report of the Joint Economic Subcommittee on International Exchange and Payments in August, 1961. I believe that they are the right terms.

Under the Joint Economic Committee's proposal, the ten or so major industrial countries—the United States, the Western European countries, Canada, and Japan—would enter into a standby agreement with the IMF to purchase up to a specified amount of IMF interest-bearing certificates for the purpose of settling deficits within the group. The total amount to be made available and its distribution among the participants under the agreement must be such that the foreseeable, justified needs of any of the countries of the group could be met for, say, up to ten years. A deficit country could apply to the IMF for a loan of the currency it needs to finance its deficit. Creditor countries would lend their currencies in exchange for IMF certificates carrying a maintenance of exchange value guarantee. The certificates would be negotiable by a creditor country in the event that it found itself in a deficit.

Deficit countries would be able to borrow with a high degree of automaticity on the basis of general rules agreed upon in advance. Surplus countries would have the obligation to lend to any and all borrowers within the group up to the limits set upon them by their agreement. Loans should be available for up to ten years. The agreement should look to the accession of additional industrial countries as they qualify by accumulating reserves.

But how can you be sure that the total reserves created by this method will be adequate? You cannot, because the agreed-upon lending limits of individual countries may not match up with actual borrowing needs in the future. For example, Germany's obligation to purchase IMF certificates may be exhausted by loans to the United States. If the United States is still in deficit to Germany at the time Italy, say, also goes into deficit with Germany, Italy will not be able to receive automatic credit under the plan from Germany.

Therefore, this standby agreement mechanism will need to be supplemented by a method of creating an additional reserve potential. This can be done in several ways. One is to provide for an automatic percentage increase in potential reserves every year or so by a predetermined increase in the amounts the member countries agree to lend. The difficulty with this method is that it fails to take account of the actual future reserve needs of particular countries, and hence may still fail to make available adequate access to reserves by them. Another method is the direct creation of additional reserves by open-market purchases—à la the Federal Reserve—by the IMF. This has the same disadvantage of possible inadequacy as the first method; worse, it exposes creditor countries to liability to give credit in amounts of great magnitude and over which they have no control. A more appropriate method would be to incorporate in the new monetary mechanism a provision that countries running persistent surpluses in their balance of payments make some percentage of that surplus available as additional credit to member countries needing it.

The proposed improved international monetary mechanism would provide something like the "elastic currency" which the Federal Reserve provides for our internal monetary system. The analogy was well stated by the Joint Economic Committee:

> One of the strengths of the domestic economy consists in its ability to adjust output to changing demand. When more automobiles are wanted, more will be produced. The same responsiveness can be found in the domestic monetary system. When more domestic reserves are "needed" by the banking system, more will normally be made available through the central banks, or, if the deficiency is felt by only some banks, then through the sale of financial assets by them to other banks whose reserves are excessive. But there seems to be no mechanism which insures the appropriate response of supply to changes in the need for international reserves. In this critical sector, chance, as it helps determine how much gold can be profitably mined, and the combination of forces that influence the balance of payments of the key currency countries, plays the predominant role in affecting the supply. The demand for reserves plays little part. There is, thus, an ever-present danger that a country's reserves will fall below the level it needs, and that its corrective actions will be injurious to the economic well-being of the free world.*

The present system of inadequate over-all reserves is an important factor in preventing an adequate free world-wide development aid program. Countries with payments deficits, like the United States, tend to cut down on their total foreign aid, and to make it more costly by "tying" it. Countries with payments surpluses, like the countries of Western Europe, shy

---

* "International Payments Imbalances and Need for Strengthening International Financial Arrangements," Report of the Subcommittee on International Exchange and Payments to the Congressional Joint Economic Committee, Aug. 23, 1961, p. 5.

away from large foreign aid programs because they look forward to an expansion in their commercial trade and do not want to reduce their reserves now. The proposed improved monetary mechanism would help the developed countries of the free world to plan foreign aid on a more sustained basis, without sudden interruptions and fluctuations due to "exchange crises."

Three objections are usually made to the proposal here discussed—that it would lead to inflation, that it would postpone necessary adjustments on the part of the debtor country, and that it would result in a loss of sovereignty. None of these objections holds water.

The Economic Advisory Council of the United States Chamber of Commerce has summarized at least two of these objections:

Some of the proposed reforms of the IMF would give it much greater power to deal with liquidity crises, but power also to inflate the supply of international monetary reserves and thereby delay needed adjustments.*

The inflation argument tends to disappear on analysis. The leading industrialized countries of the free world today recognize the danger of domestic inflation. They have all shown a considerable determination to use fiscal, monetary, and direct methods of preventing domestic inflation. There are enough evils in domestic inflation to compel a government to act against it without the additional goad of a balance-of-payments deficit. On the other hand, if a country's problem is not inflation but unemployment and stagnation, exposing it unprotected to a balance-of-payments crisis is going to force the country to take action which will accentuate its domestic troubles.

As for the argument that the provision of adequate reserves

* "International Payments and Exchange Rates," United States Chamber of Commerce, 1963.

will retard needed adjustments, just the opposite seems closer to the fact. These needed adjustments, as we have seen, take several years to come about. Adequate reserves, therefore, can alone make the adjustments possible.

A third argument is "loss of sovereignty": today a country can decide whether to keep its reserves in gold, dollars, or sterling, while under the proposal an increasing amount would be kept in IMF certificates.

This loss of sovereignty is more apparent than real. European countries today keep their reserves in dollars and in sterling largely because they have to, not because they want to. An IMF certificate would give a guarantee against devaluation which they now lack. An adequate international monetary mechanism would, in fact, restore real sovereignty to each country over its power to grow economically, its trade policy, and its military and economic assistance programs.

We now enjoy neither of the advantages that would come from an adequate international monetary mechanism. The dollar and other currencies are not adequately protected against destabilizing outflows.

Nor is there a rational method for increasing world international reserves in proper amount.

Why did we fail for so long to work for an adequate monetary mechanism? The answer seems to be that foreign central bankers and financial officials prefer the present system, which gives them a considerable toehold on American policy.

The June, 1963, report of the Bank for International Settlements, which speaks for all the central bankers of Europe, vigorously opposed a new international monetary mechanism:

Some proposals for new forms of international liquidity have been aimed at relieving the pressure on the U.S. gold stock . . . [but] designing schemes to make the access to liquidity easier will not solve this problem. The only real solution is [for the United States] to eliminate the external deficit. One must ask . . . whether the corrective measures . . . have been too limited.

The BIS report approves of the proposed United States Federal Reserve and Treasury cooperation with European central banks, calling it much preferable to "any mechanistic scheme for increasing liquidity."

The new Managing Director of the IMF (succeeding the late Per Jacobsson) is Pierre-Paul Schweitzer, who was deputy governor of the Bank of France before coming to the IMF. He, too, reflects the views of central bankers. In an interview in the July 6, 1963, *Economist,* he in effect ruled out making the IMF into an adequate international monetary mechanism:

Schweitzer: At the present time countries are just not willing to surrender the degree of sovereignty that would be needed if the fund were to be given central banking powers.

Question: Leaving aside the now rather irrelevant question of whether there is a shortage of total liquidity—Professor Triffin holds that the financing of the American deficit has actually created an excess—do you see any present strain on the international monetary system as now organised, a strain that would require new developments of the international credit mechanism?

Schweitzer: No, I don't really see any such strain. Not at present. The basic trend in the American balance of payments should now be favourable. Admittedly, the trade balance might be adversely affected a little by economic recovery; but, against this, it should be possible to reduce the outflow of capital, for here corrective measures can be applied. Yes, I would say that the suggestion of a tightening of American monetary policy, combined with an easing of fiscal policy to allow larger budget deficits, seems pretty sensible to me.

For a long time, these chill words from across the Atlantic were apparently sufficient to deter the Administration from even suggesting steps toward an adequate monetary mechanism. Indeed, when suggestions for reform of the international monetary system were made by European sources as by the United Kingdom's Reginald Maudling in September, 1962, the Treasury outspokenly exhibited lack of interest in them.

Clearly, if we rely on central bankers and finance ministers, we will never have an adequate monetary mechanism. Bold innovation is not a way to succeed as a central banker or finance minister. This is too bad. As Prof. Harry G. Johnson of the University of Chicago told the annual meeting of the Midwest Economic Association at St. Louis on Apr. 25, 1963:

Central bankers are elected by no democratic process, and their function in economic organization is to serve the interests of money rather than of people; what is worse, they are usually endowed with a constitutional inability to appreciate that the welfare of people can vary inversely with the welfare of money, and prone to confuse monetary morality with sound economics. It therefore seems to me extremely dangerous for the Administration to repose so much confidence in the wisdom of central bankers to manage the world's monetary affairs by formal or informal arrangements among themselves, and a strong point of criticism of its international economic policy that it has contented itself with shoring up an inherently unstable monetary system rather than with pressing for adoption of a more stable one.

At the July 8, 1963, Joint Economic Committee hearings, I expressed my regret to Secretary of the Treasury Dillon that we were letting Europe's financial authorities scare us out of even asking them to do the necessary:

Representative Reuss: I recognize that the report of the Bank for International Settlements which you have just mentioned did indeed pooh-pooh the idea of any new initiative in international monetary cooperation. But I would want to throw out this thought. The BIS is made up of the central bankers and monetary authorities of the various countries, and I am wondering if the subject of the economic health of the free world is not too important to be left entirely to the central bankers. If it is in order for President Kennedy, for example, to publicly ask our friends and neighbors to buy the idea of nuclear armed merchant ships, would it not be equally in order for him to go over the heads of the central bankers and ask the democratically elected leaders of our friends and neighbors to all put their shoulders to the wheel and come up with the kind of international monetary arrangement which will end the present situation, where we can't put our own economic house in order? What would you say to that?

Secretary Dillon: Well, I think we can put our own economic house in order even doing the things that are necessary to move toward balance-of-payments equilibrium. As far as the central bankers of Europe are concerned, all of them work very closely with their elected governments, in some cases constitutionally they are the national authority for carrying out foreign exchange policy rather than the finance ministry.

It is time that we disentangled ourselves from the embraces of Europe's central bankers and finance ministers. So long as they continue to "finance" us on a 90-day basis, they can continue to call the tune on our economy. Recently this has been to tell us in one breath that we must restore full employment and adequate growth, and in the next that the way to do this is by having tight money.

Our future, and that of the free world, is too important to be left to the technicians on either side of the Atlantic. Fortunately, there are now indications that the Treasury is prepared to move toward a more adequate international monetary mechanism. It will not lack for help abroad. In the United Kingdom, he can expect help from both Conservative Chancellor of the Exchequer Reginald Maudling, and from Harold Wilson, leader of the Labour Party. In Germany, Erhard, Brandt, and Mende, leaders of the Christian Democratic, Social Democratic, and Free Democratic parties, are also sympathetic.

Concerted action by the leaders of the industrialized free world nations is what is needed to get moving forward in the monetary field. Hopefully, this can emerge from the "study" commissioned at the IMF's annual meeting in Washington in October, 1963. Unanimity of the key countries is desirable. But we should go ahead without the dissidents in any event.

A monetary solution is interwoven with the accomplishment of all our other great priorities. Trade cannot expand in its absence. Aid is dependent upon it. Full employment is blocked without it. Furthermore, agreement on a new monetary mechanism is the best way to political cohesion.

The Joint Economic Committee urged that we move toward such an agreement back in 1961. There is no time to lose.

Down with the deficit, up with a new mechanism

So what should the United States do about its balance-of-payments deficit, and the lack of an adequate international monetary mechanism?

Foreign central bankers keep insisting that the free world cannot have a new international monetary mechanism until the United States "puts its house in order" and eliminates its payments deficit. The trouble with this is that the best way of putting our house in order would be under a new international monetary mechanism. Without such a mechanism, we may be forced to take undesirable steps in the effort to eliminate our deficit.

Conversely, some academic economists advise—quite properly—of the necessity for creating an adequate international monetary mechanism at once, but are lackadaisical as to when, if ever, we are supposed to bring our payments into balance. The trouble here is that other countries cannot really be expected to join in an agreement for an adequate monetary mechanism if it appears that its main purpose is to finance a permanent American payments deficit.

We should reject both of these alternatives. What we ought to do *now* is to move vigorously toward a new international monetary mechanism, and at the same time to take more decisive measures to achieve a prompt payments balance. As we try to expand our exports and otherwise increase our receipts, we must at the same time cut down—in ways which will do the least national harm—the main items of outflow such as capital investment abroad, military defense, and untied foreign aid. Just as soon as our measures to expand receipts succeed sufficiently to bring us into surplus, the restrictions imposed on the payments side can and should be relaxed.

CHAPTER FOUR

Our Aid Program:
The Rich and the Poor

> The ability to wipe out poverty is perhaps the most important fact of our time. Hundreds of millions of people, whose forebears patiently accepted lives of misery, are involved in what has been referred to so often as "the revolution of rising expectations." What had been a distant dream has now become a passionate demand.
>
> Paul G. Hoffman

As a people we try to live by the Golden Rule, to do unto others as we would have them do unto us. Thus the act of helping the developing peoples of Asia, Africa, and Latin America to obtain some of the good things of life for themselves would seem only to be doing what comes naturally. We are the rich, and they are the poor. Because of their poverty, they are beset by illiteracy, disease, and malnutrition.

Without outside help, they cannot generate the capital which alone will enable them to advance, rather than to fall into chaos or communism. With help from the outside, the chances are good that the developing countries can rise from their poverty and attain a greater measure of justice, freedom, and dignity for each human being. With a stake in the future, they will be more ready and able to defend themselves against tyranny and inhumanity, from without or within, and to take their places in a free and peaceful world.

104

Yet, 17 years after the start of our aid program, a 1963 Gallup Poll showed that only 58 per cent of the American people supported foreign aid. To hear the annual debates in Congress on the aid authorization and appropriation, one would think that the support was even less than this thin majority.

Why should this be so? Why should a country which purports to live by the Christian ethic find itself so badly split on whether it is right for us to cast our bread upon the waters? The unpopularity of the aid program stems from three main causes.

First, to the extent that the aid program has been sold to the American people as a method of buying friends, it has obviously failed. The foes of foreign aid, though they err in proclaiming the quest for popularity as the goal of the foreign aid program, are right when they point out that you can't buy friends.* When we helped Nkrumah of Ghana, what did he do but to close down our information offices? No sooner did Indonesia's Sukarno request of us an increase in economic grant aid than he turned around and bought $1 billion worth of Russian military hardware. Tito of Yugoslavia took our

* As Robert E. Asher of the Brookings Institution points out, Russians and Chinese might well ask variations of the same questions asked in the United States. "Why," they might ask, "are we Communists squandering scarce resources in Egypt, Iraq, Yemen and India? Egypt locks up its communists and vies with Yugoslavia for leadership of the neutral bloc; Iraq has *not* gone communist; Yemen is hopelessly reactionary; India, that ungrateful nation, played a key role in rescuing the United Nations Congo operation at the time Russia most wanted to torpedo it. Why, moreover, is Russia offering India planes that might be used against China? Why are stadia being built with communist help in Indonesia and roads in Afghanistan, when housing is so desperately needed in Moscow and Peking? What does Guinea mean by accepting our aid and then kicking out our ambassador? Why don't Russia and China co-operate and share the aid burden sensibly instead of competing with each other in a number of countries?" See Asher, *Multilateral versus Bilateral Aid: An Old Controversy Revisited,* reprinted from *International Organization,* Autumn 1962, p. 706 (Brookings Reprint No. 66).

Public Law 480 food shipments, and then proceeded to vote in the United Nations with the Soviet bloc and against us on more than two-thirds of the 154 roll-call votes between 1958 and 1962. He is on solid psychological ground who asks: "I don't know why you hate me. I haven't done anything for you recently."

In the second place, even if we look at the aid program in terms of its proper goal—not to win a popularity contest, but to help emerging peoples to help themselves—we see that the results of our aid program have been tantalizingly slow. By and large, developing peoples and their territories have been kept from falling into Communist hands. But they are still desperately poor, almost as poor as they were in 1950.

India, it is true, has over this period increased its industrial production by 100 per cent and its food production by 50 per cent, though much of this has been soaked up in population growth. Taiwan, Israel, Greece, Nigeria, Costa Rica have likewise made impressive progress. But for the developing countries as a whole, a man's average annual income remains at about the $100 level of 1950. Thus many thoughtful Americans question the aid program's basis.

The reasons for the agonizingly slow progress are both that the aid we have given the developing countries is less than we had thought, and that their need was greater than we had thought.

True, since the end of World War II, we have disbursed abroad around $100 billion in grants and loans (more than $12 billion of which has been paid back). But of this total, nearly one-third was given to rehabilitate war-torn Europe under the Marshall Plan and similar programs, rather than to the developing countries. The strength of Western Europe today pays tribute to those programs.

Another one-third went to support anti-Communist military forces in Europe, Korea, Formosa, Viet Nam, and elsewhere around the globe. Our military aid program to some 60 countries has played a major role in enabling them to stem the advance of Communist aggression.

Another one-sixth of our total foreign aid expenditure was in the form of surplus farm commodities, and in Export-Import Bank loans to finance export sales of American industrial products.

This has left around $16 billion—one-sixth of our total foreign aid—to help develop Asia, Africa, and Latin America. Most of this $16 billion development aid through 1962 went to a score of the 80-odd countries asking for development assistance. In the Far East, the principal beneficiaries were Korea, $2.1 billion; Viet Nam, $1.5 billion; Formosa, $1.3 billion; Indochina (pre-1954), $826 million; Laos, $290 million; Cambodia, $248 million; Indonesia, $243 million. India got $1.4 billion; Turkey, $1.2 billion; Pakistan, $1.1 billion; Greece, $1 billion; Afghanistan, $134 million. In the Middle East, Iran got $568 million; Israel, $419 million; Jordan, $274 million; Egypt, $126 million. In Africa, Morocco got $240 million; Tunisia, $165 million. In Latin America, Chile got $219 million; Bolivia, $189 million; Brazil, $138 million. Since the largest beneficiaries were those receiving military assistance, much of this aid was more "defense support" than pure economic aid.

The other 60-odd countries of the underdeveloped world have received altogether but a few hundred million. The lion's share went to countries which happen to lie on the periphery of the Communist empire.

Progress has been slow not simply because the aid has been spread so thin, but because the aided are so poor. Most of them have vast resources of manpower—but these are largely untapped. Many have great natural resources—but these are unexploited, and the capital needed for such exploitation must come from elsewhere. All want roads, ports, schools, hospitals, infant industries, more productive agriculture, better health, honest and competent governments—but their stifling poverty prevents a sudden evolution into the modern world.

We Americans would do well to recall where we were a century ago. The average American's income then, measured in today's dollars, was some $300 a year—the same as that of a South American today. Three-fifths of our workers were on the farm. One-fifth of our people could not read or write. It took the United States a century to reach our unparalleled prosperity of the Sixties.

Modern technology and the revolutionary spirit abroad in Asia, Africa, and Latin America may make things move faster. But the march up from poverty will surely continue to be their main business for the rest of the 20th century. Results will continue to be slow, and the impatient American will continue to be exasperated.

A third reason why our foreign aid program enjoys such a slim margin of support lies in its *governmental* nature. Foreign aid is something a citizen in Dubuque pays for in his tax return; Congress then votes the program and appropriations for it; the money is presumably spent somewhere, although the Executive Branch is forbidden by law to propagandize on how well it may have been spent. What the citizen hears, mostly, is that the schools and hospitals he needs back home can't be had because his tax money is going into foreign aid—an argument that overlooks an underemployed economy that could provide *both* schools and hospitals *and* foreign aid.

The wonder of foreign aid—oversold as "buying friends," disappointing in its results, and remote from the people who pay for it—is that it can command even a 58 per cent support.

The 1963 course of the foreign aid bill through Congress reflects the program's uncertain support. Once again, the bill moved with the stylized certainty of a Japanese Noh drama.

The Administration at the start of the year asked a $4.9 billion authorization about equally divided between economic and military aid. Then came the report of the study committee headed by Gen. Lucius Clay asserting that "we are over-extended in resources and undercompensated in results," and that we are "trying to do too much for too many too soon." This caused the Administration to reduce its request to $4.5 billion. The House Foreign Affairs Committee, after four months of hearings, recommended an authorization of $4.1 billion. The House reduced this to $3.5 billion. On the Senate side the story was much the same. The Senate Foreign Relations Committee reported out a bill authorizing $4.2 billion. This was reduced to $3.7 billion on the floor. In Conference, the two bodies, as usual, split the difference. There would then follow the second act of the drama, in which the appropriation which had just been authorized was subjected to an even further cut in the amount allocated to foreign aid. Once again, a divided and uncertain public opinion, reflected in the Congress, had produced an aid contribution inadequate for the task.

Let us look at the arithmetic of development for the almost 1½ billion people of the developing world.

The Economic and Social Council of the United Nations has estimated that the underdeveloped countries will need a minimum of $10 billion to $12 billion a year in capital from the free world for many years to come if they are to start generating their own growth. In the early Sixties, economic aid to the developing countries from the United States (the grants, loans, and technical assistance in the regular foreign aid legislation, plus Peace Corps, export credits, and Food for Peace in separate bills) came to around $3 to $4 billion annually; from the other developed countries, around $2.5 billion; with private investment added, the total is between $6 billion and

$8 billion. This leaves a deficiency of from $2 to $6 billion annually between the minimum needs of the developing countries and what they actually receive.

The problem for the advanced nations, then, is how to fill the $2–$6 billion annual gap between present programs and present needs. This is the great challenge which Barbara Ward has defined as:

. . . to remove the work of world development from the subsidiary attention of the wealthy nations and to make it the central theme of their diplomacy, their international relationships, their philosophy of world order, their hopes for a future in which not only groups and nations but the entire human race can make this small planet into a habitable home.*

It is imperative that the United States do what it can to see that capital needs—human and material—of the developing countries are met. Much progress has been made in the last three years. But much more needs to be done. Our agenda must include the following: (1) assuring a prosperous free world community; (2) inducing other advanced nations to contribute more; (3) resisting the tendency to carve up the developing world into spheres of influence; (4) enforcing for all we are worth criteria of self-help for the developing countries; (5) upgrading that part of our diplomatic corps which administers foreign aid; and (6) making foreign aid concrete rather than abstract by involving in it the broadest spectrum of the American people.

Assuring a prosperous free world community

An across-the-board program for the economic prosperity of the free world through expanded trade, a modernized international monetary mechanism, and maximum economic growth in the developed countries is the best possible way of assuring

* *Restless Nations: A Study of World Tensions and Development,* Council on World Tensions, New York (1962), p. 67.

that the developing countries will obtain the capital needed for their development.

The liberalized, nondiscriminatory expanded world trade which must be our goal at the GATT negotiations can help the developing countries to expand their current export earnings of around $30 billion a year—a large sum when contrasted with the $2–$6 billion capital gap. It can make each of the developed countries more prosperous, and hence better able to buy the goods of the developing countries, and to contribute to their capital by foreign aid. This will require, as has been suggested in Chapter 2, a decision on the part of the advanced nations to accept not only exports of raw materials from the developing nations, but their manufactured goods as well—textiles and apparel, simple machinery and manufactured food products. It will require that the advanced nations allow an interim period to the developing nations in which they may retain tariffs of their own to enable their infant industries to get started. It will require advanced countries, such as some of those of continental Europe which impose heavy sales taxes on tropical products like tea and coffee, to lighten the tax so as to increase their consumption of such products.

A vexing trade problem is presented by countries whose exports are dominated by a single raw material—Ghana and Nigeria in cocoa, Tanganyika in pyrethrum, Malaya in tin, Chile in copper, Brazil in coffee, Liberia in bauxite, Somalia in bananas. Countries which depend for their foreign exchange on a single commodity find themselves devastated when the price drops. International commodity agreements designed to control the production and maintain the price of a commodity have been attempted for wheat, sugar, and zinc. But commodity agreements are no panacea. Our own American experience with them in agricultural price supports indicates the enormous difficulties and dislocations. Their administration, particularly as between the advanced and developing countries, could be a source of endless friction. Thus they are a dubious form of foreign aid, far inferior to techniques designed to induce one-commodity countries to diversify their production.

As we have seen in Chapter 3, a modern international monetary mechanism is essential if the advanced countries are to make their foreign aid programs more nearly dependent upon their real wealth and capacity to produce, rather than upon the temporary status of their foreign exchange reserves.

Full employment in the United States, and an adequate growth rate, discussed in Chapters 5 and 6, would be the easiest solvent for the $2–$6 billion gap. If we fully used our manpower and our productive equipment, we could add another $30–$60 billion a year to our gross national product. It would surely be no hardship to find an additional $1–$3 billion a year for added economic aid out of such totals.

Progress in reducing cold war tensions which would make it possible for us to reduce our present $50-billion-plus expenditures on armaments would likewise make possible a "painless" increase in foreign aid.

Inducing other advanced nations to contribute more

We have made some progress in the last three years in inducing other advanced nations to share in bearing the burden of foreign aid, but not enough. The creation of the Organization for Economic Cooperation and Development has given us a forum in which we are able to plead, with some success, for a more equitable sharing.

Currently the United States is still giving more than one-half of the free world's foreign economic aid. In terms of percentages of gross national product devoted to economic aid, we and the other advanced nations each give about the same— two-thirds of 1 per cent. The average is made up of some, like France, which give more than 1 per cent; and others, like Canada, whose contributions are considerably lower than the average. Of course, percentages are tricky: the Europeans argue that the United States should give a *greater* percentage of its GNP, because our GNP per capita is much higher than theirs; we argue that our vastly greater defense expenditures entitle us to give *less*.

The type of contribution is relevant, too. A large part of our aid program is in grants or "soft loans"—long-term low-interest loans which take into account the future difficulties the debtor country will have in repaying them. Other advanced nations, notably Germany, have a policy of making "hard loans," those for relatively short terms and at relatively high rates. Recently, Germany has been making softer development loans, such as the 1963 loan to India at 3 per cent interest, with a seven-year no-interest "grace period." And Britain has cut its interest rate on certain development loans.

Again, the development activities of other advanced nations tend to be concentrated on their former colonies, particularly in the case of France and Great Britain; aid is on a "tied" basis, requiring the proceeds to be spent in the donor country.

Despite progress, therefore, we must continue our pressure for more foreign aid contributions by the advanced nations of the free world, on terms that make them truly aid rather than mere commercial transactions, to as wide a group of beneficiaries as possible, and on an "untied" basis as much as possible.

So much for development aid by the advanced nations of the free world. What about aid from the Sino-Soviet bloc? Since 1955, this bloc has committed $6.3 billion, $4.8 billion in economic loans and $1.5 billion in military loans. Since only a fraction of the commitments have so far been honored, it seems unlikely that the free world can look to the Communist bloc for any significant help in meeting the capital requirements of the developing world.

Resisting spheres of influence

Our aid program would do well to pay no heed to those voices which suggest that the developing world be divided into spheres of influence by the advanced nations. Sometimes this suggestion comes as a gloss on the "dumbbell" concept of a partnership between a strong Europe and a strong America: let the Europeans keep Africa and various other former colonial territories as their bailiwick, and let America accept as her special province Latin America and the Pacific.

The proposal crops up in the thinking of the Common Marketers, who advocate special privileges and ties for the former French and Belgian colonies in Africa. It pervades the report of the Clay Committee:

The new countries of Africa in most cases have maintained close ties with the former metropoles without impairment of their full independence, and the latter in turn have displayed considerable willingness to help meet the assistance needs of these young nations. The Committee regards Africa as an area where the Western European countries should logically bear most of the necessary aid burden. In fact, this is proving to be the case. Almost all nations formerly under French aegis are now receiving heavy French assistance, largely in grants. We welcome this present arrangement, based on past relationship, and trust it will continue. Similarly, the new nations formerly under British rule should look largely to the United Kingdom for economic assistance, and we hope that this experienced nation will continue to provide it. The new Overseas Development Fund of the European Economic Community also should prove a major source of help.*

What is needed in the free world today is universality and interdependence, not parochialism and dependence. Just as out of date as the concept of an autarchic, nationalistic Big Six in Europe is the concept of the Six and the United States dividing up the rest of the world into spheres of influence.

The United States has made great strides in Africa in recent years. While our foreign aid expenditures in Africa are currently less than one-third of Europe's, we are established as a

* The Committee to Strengthen the Security of the Free World, *The Scope and Distribution of United States Military and Economic Assistance Programs,* Department of State, March 20, 1963, p. 9.

"presence" there. We have elevated African affairs to an Assistant Secretaryship in the Department of State, and have appointed the energetic former Governor of Michigan, G. Mennen Williams, to the post. Unlike the French and the Germans and the British and the Italians and the Belgians, we are free of the onus of colonialism in Africa. We have no axe to grind for exclusive channels of trade.

Africa, for her part, needs not only our economic aid but exposure to our democratic institutions. A resource as yet hardly touched is the awakening affinity between our 20 million American Negro citizens and the land of their forefathers. The leaders of new Africa want an American presence on their continent. They admire our democracy, our business acumen, our skill in agriculture and education and reclamation.

Equally, it would be a tragic mistake for the United States to accept Latin America and the Pacific littoral as our almost exclusive concern. The dominant civilization of Latin America is European. European investment and European culture are badly needed there, and in Japan as well.

Criteria of self-help

Both Congress and the Administration have for several years been moving toward "strings" to our aid, so that it will not be wasted by countries which do little or nothing to help themselves. We first applied these criteria in Latin America under the Alliance for Progress. They increasingly govern our over-all aid program.

Does the country have a long-range development plan, so that it can use its native and imported resources effectively? Particularly if the country is a smaller one, does it adopt a regional approach, or does it selfishly insist that it must produce everything within its own borders? Is the system of taxation a reasonable one, and is it honestly administered? Is land tenure such as not only to encourage efficiency, but to give the individual peasant a stake in his future? Are the country's foreign exchange controls such as to discourage luxury imports and the flight of its capital? Is there sufficient emphasis on village development, and on education? Is the government one stemming in some degree from the consent of the governed? Does it deal fairly with private capital investment?

The Kennedy Administration has not been squeamish about curtailing aid to countries which stray too far from these criteria. In Ceylon, we stopped our aid when the government expropriated foreign oil properties in 1961, and reinstated aid when compensation was provided. When a military junta took over the government of Peru in 1962, we suspended our aid program except for surplus food; the program was reinstated when the junta permitted the restoration of civil government and free elections. In 1963, we curtailed aid to Brazil because needed fiscal reforms were not being undertaken.

Political or strategic considerations, of course, may require that the criteria be relaxed occasionally. As Ambassador to India Chester Bowles, himself an author of the criteria, has observed:

> There is nothing in [the criteria] that requires us to be foolhardy. Specific situations may occasionally cause us to throw away the book, to exercise our own ad hoc judgment and temporarily to relax our pressures for reform.

Perhaps the best thing about the new criteria is that they diminish our temptation toward grandiose projects which glorify the vanity of a country's ruler, but have little impact on its people. Our record until recently was not always edifying. We supplied Ethiopia with jet fighter planes because the emperor wanted the attendant prestige. We unloaded unnecessary navies on various Latin American republics. In Liberia, one of the poorest countries in Africa, we built a palace for President William V. S. Tubman.

In Cambodia, we built the Khmer-American Friendship Highway from the capital at Phnom Penh over the mountains and through the jungle to the new French-built port, formerly Kompong Som, renamed Sihanoukville in honor of Cambodia's ruler, Prince Sihanouk. It was at the Prince's insistence that the magnificent highway was built, but beyond his personal feelings of gratification it is difficult to see how the road has helped Cambodia. Parts of the highway have since been used for growing rice; its shoulder is used by carts pulled by water buffalo.

While such projects as the United Nations Mekong River project bring Cambodia and her neighbors, Thailand and Viet Nam, together in mutual assistance, the Friendship Highway drives them apart. In the days of French rule, the principal ports for Cambodia were Bangkok in Thailand and Saigon in Viet Nam. An independent road and port is the way to autarchy, not interdependence.

Ironically, while the United States was constructing this superhighway through the jungles, the Soviet Union was building a modern, 500-bed hospital in Phnom Penh. Thus imperialist Russia appears in Cambodia as the benign practitioner of the healing arts, while the United States, seeking only to help other peoples to help themselves, appears bearing that prime symbol of military imperialism since Roman times, the strategic highway.

A troublesome question is whether we should condition our aid upon the recipient country's adopting something like our own political and economic systems. Our political system is representative democracy, based upon debate, the civil liberties, free elections. Our economic system is capitalism, based upon private enterprise and the market economy, with its rough edges smoothed by welfare legislation.

There is no denying that political democracy is a frail plant in Asia, Africa, and Latin America. From Pakistan to Ghana, from Indonesia to Ecuador, the Western model of parliamentary democracy has given way to more or less authoritarian forms of government. Authoritarianism, often backed by the military, came about because the country's divisions of tribe or caste or religion were too deep-seated, or because too many of its citizens resisted the imposition of taxes or the reform of land tenures, or because the chasm between the educated new governors and the illiterate masses was too great.

There was no cushion of time, as in democratic models of Western Europe and the United States, for democracy to grow in pace with national income and education and administrative expertise.

We cannot, therefore, adopt as a criterion of our aid that the recipient have a Western-style parliamentary democracy. What we can and should ask of an authoritarian government is that it temper its authoritarianism with a regard for human rights, such as the right to a free press, to habeas corpus, to fair treatment for minorities; that it move toward free elections at least for an executive; and that its economic and social goals favor the great mass of the people rather than the privileged few.

As parliamentary democracy has given way to a strong-executive one-party system in many countries, so has collectivism—government ownership, government planning, government regulation—quite generally characterized the economies of the developing countries.

There are at least three reasons for this collectivist emphasis. Much of the development would be in the public sector even in our own country—ports, roads, schools, hospitals, dams, irrigation projects.

Secondly, private capital simply is not available for much industrial development which we have regarded as traditionally private. Domestic capital runs off to a safe deposit box in Switzerland; foreign capital is scared off by the unstable politics of the developing country, and finds investment opportunities at home more profitable.

In the third place, the word "socialism," anathema in the United States, has charisma throughout much of the developing world. Under the Marshall Plan, we did not allow the nationalization of various industries in Britain and France, and their emphasis on economic planning, to restrain our aid program. We must be similarly tolerant of the desire of developing peoples to choose their own forms of economic organization.

But we have a right and a duty to insist that the country's economic institutions, however organized, be efficiently conducted. We should not sponsor a steel mill in every country that wants one, though it may lack both the resources and the market for economical production. We should continue to insist that developing countries keep their commitments to foreign private capital. And we should be as receptive as possible toward mixed elements in their economies, including public corporations which instead of being monopolies compete with each other, cooperatives, and small business units.

Upgrading our foreign aid corps

The Kennedy Administration has made real progress in the administration of foreign aid. AID Administrator David Bell is surely one of the most effective men on the New Frontier. For the last ten years, we have had as our aid administrators Harold Stassen, who wanted to be President; John B. Hollister, who didn't believe in foreign aid; James Riddleberger, who wanted to get back into the diplomatic corps; Fowler Hamilton, who wanted to get back to Wall Street; and Henry Labouisse, a gentle soul with no stomach for the infighting of the Washington bureaucracy. Bell combines a penchant for efficiency, enough for any economy-minded Congressman, with a real belief in the possibilities of foreign aid.

The field operations of foreign aid have also been improved. Administration in each country has been centered under the American ambassador rather than left as a semi-independent aid satrapy.

More progress needs to be made in dignifying and professionalizing our foreign aid representatives. They now have neither the security nor the status of Foreign Service Officers. We will have difficulty attracting and keeping able people until they do.

Involving Americans in foreign aid

The fundamental American political problem with foreign aid, then, is that we have to stay with it for a long time to come and increase it as we can. With the present split between those favoring and those opposing foreign aid, this is difficult to achieve.

How do you increase the proportion among us of those favoring foreign aid? Only, I believe, by giving more Americans some personal involvement with it, some concrete and immediate role, rather than simply the abstract and remote role of paying taxes to support it.

If we could make of our foreign aid an all-American program, touching every facet of American life, we could begin to bring about this involvement. Look at some of the elements of our American life which could have a role, or a much greater role, in helping developing peoples:

Business has already had a long and productive history in developing areas, from Aramco in Saudi Arabia, to Creole in Venezuela, to Cities Service in Libya, to United Fruit in Central America, to Kaiser Aluminum in Ghana, to Anaconda in Chile, to Sears, Roebuck in Brazil. Large-scale investment by American business is, of course, going to be dictated by economic considerations. But an American business "presence" in a dozen new developing countries could be as much a part of corporate citizenship as supporting the home town symphony or community chest. David Rockefeller's suggestion for spreading American management skills abroad deserves wide support.

Labor unions have played a great role already in foreign aid, and can play a greater one. The AFL-CIO spends almost one-fourth of its total budget in assisting trade unions in the developing countries.

Foundations like the Ford, Rockefeller, and Phelps-Stokes foundations have conducted economic resource studies, management and scientific training, and a host of other assistance activities in developing countries. But the surface has hardly been scratched.

Cooperatives have already had signal success overseas, in coffee in Tanganyika, cotton in Uganda, chicken-raising in Ghana, in the heifer program in Colombia, Kenya, Liberia, Ethiopia, and Turkey.

Financial institutions, such as banks, credit unions, and savings-and-loan institutions already have a foothold. The United States savings-and-loan principle is being used to provide low-cost housing in Peru and Venezuela. American bankers are helping to train their opposite numbers in Nigeria and Liberia.

The *communications industry* can help, too, as the Radio Corporation of America is helping Nigeria create a TV system.

Universities and colleges already staff overseas universities and train students from the developing countries in the United

States. The Agency for International Development currently has contracts with some 103 American universities and colleges.

Religious and charitable organizations have already played an important role. They range from medical missionaries to CARE, which has received more than $150 million in voluntary contributions. Involving American Negro churches with African development has hardly been attempted.

Professional societies, such as those of physicians and lawyers, could channel retired professional people for voluntary short-term service in the developing countries.

Agricultural organizations, such as the Farm Bureau, the National Grange, and the Farmers Union, could greatly increase their foreign operations. The large-scale introduction of hybrid corn to Africa, for example, could mean a vast improvement in diet.

States and cities could well "adopt" an "opposite number" in the developing countries, as Minneapolis has "adopted" Santiago, Chile. Developing administrators could intern in American cities to learn budgeting or police administration or public health or purchasing; our own public officials could be made available for sabbaticals in the developing areas.

Voluntary organizations of all types are needed. Rotary International has recently been giving small-business clinics in Tanganyika and Burma on market surveys and inventory control. The League of Women Voters, the American Association of University Women, or the General Federation of Women's Clubs could give demonstration projects in how women may participate in a democracy.

Almost every one of these categories has made tentative beginnings at helping the developing peoples. These beginnings now must be enormously expanded, and the activities made part of a nationwide program, a giant "community sing," which could be heard all over Asia, Africa, and Latin America. Much good would come of it if President Johnson could call a long conference in Washington of the thousands of Americans representing these categories to block out that kind of all-American program.*

As observers could be present representatives of governmental agencies interested in foreign aid—AID, Food for Peace, the Peace Corps, the Export-Import Bank; the various international organizations, including the United Nations and the World Bank; participants from Congress. Representatives of the developing countries might be present, too, to indicate the kinds of help they could receive from these thousands of voluntary sources.

I know that all this sounds like a Donnybrook, but out of it could come a new aspect of aid which would involve directly millions of Americans. The nongovernmental portions could supplement, in a very humane way, the necessary core of governmental grants, loans, and technical assistance. A government clearing-house could maintain a perpetual inventory of America's voluntary developmental resources. Most important of all, the chances of obtaining adequate and continuing Congressional support for the governmental portion of the total program would be measurably enhanced as the number of Americans personally involved with the developing countries increased—whether as members of a farm or labor organization, stockholders or employees of a business, contribu-

---

* Back in 1960, before the Peace Corps was born, we convened a conference at the Capitol in Washington of some sixty religious, charitable, business, labor, and civic organizations concerned with developing countries. From the give-and-take and the milling emerged the Peace Corps concept.

tors to a church or charitable organization, citizens of a city, alumni of a university, or whatever.

What Jefferson said in 1826 will still seem true to the majority of Americans:

All eyes are opened, or opening, to the rights of man. The general spread of the light of science has already laid open to every view the palpable truth, that the mass of mankind has not been born with saddles on their backs, nor a favored few booted and spurred, ready to ride them legitimately, by the grace of God.

CHAPTER FIVE

Unemployment amid Affluence

There was no unemployment in heaven,
We worked steady all through the year,
We always had food for the children,
We never were haunted by fear.
Joe Glazer, *The Mill Was Made of Marble* (1947)

America's no. one economic problem

A giant economy with huge reserve strength—but with an apparent inability to use all its strength. A growing economy—but one which has suffered frequent recessions and failed in recent years to match its own past growth performance or that of other industrial nations. A prosperous economy—but one marred by substantial poverty and a persistently high level of unemployment. These are the elements of America's major domestic economic problem for which a solution is long overdue. The delay stems from our failure to understand the problem rather than from indifference concerning its consequences. In this chapter, I shall try to define the problem and its causes. In Chapter 6, I shall outline some of the responsibilities of the Federal government in solving the problem.

AFFLUENCE BUT . . .

The average levels of consumption and well-being in this country are unparalleled either in our own history or in the rest of the world. Our 1962 per capita national income of more than $2,400 was about 50 per cent larger than that of

Sweden or Canada, twice that of prosperous Britain, West Germany, or France, four times that of Italy, and six times that of Japan. Americans spend on food only 19 per cent of their total consumer spending, compared to 30 to 40 per cent in Western Europe; 50 to 60 per cent in the Soviet Union; and 80 to 90 per cent in the poorest countries of the world.

Apart from being the best fed and clothed people in the world, we have a huge share of many of the world's conveniences and luxuries. Well over half the world's telephones and TV sets and 60 per cent of its automobiles are in the United States. Over half of all families and individuals living alone in the United States own their own homes. More than a fifth of all young Americans aged 18 to 24 attend colleges and universities—a far higher proportion than in any other country. In 1962, 930,000 Americans spent over $1.2 billion traveling to Europe and the Mediterranean at an average cost of about $1,300 per traveler.

We are not likely to endanger this economy of abundance by giving ourselves up to the sybaritic life. We make a virtue out of work, and we are thrifty enough to assure a steady flow of savings for future growth. We honor inventiveness, and we encourage innovation. We think highly of "entrepreneurship" —that indispensable ingredient without which the free enterprise system could not work. In short, as a people we continue to have the habits and qualities we need to maintain economic progress.

Until recently, our good fortune made us look with unseeing eyes at our palpable economic shortcomings. We jumped to the conclusion that poverty and high unemployment were largely things of the past. When Madison Avenue told us that our main problem was to learn how to live graciously amid plenty, and to leaven our avidity for taller tail fins with an appreciation for the finer (nonmaterial) things of life, we listened.

But the stubborn fact is that mass poverty still exists in the United States, and the rate of unemployment has been growing slowly but inexorably for at least a decade.

MASS POVERTY

President Roosevelt epitomized the mass poverty of the Thirties by saying that "one-third of a nation" was "ill-housed, ill-clad, and ill-nourished." We are better off now, but we are nowhere near eliminating poverty. Somewhere between one-fifth and one-fourth of our population are subsisting on incomes which cannot provide minimal levels of food, shelter, medical care, and other bare essentials.

For example, Keyserling,* using Department of Commerce figures on incomes and Department of Labor studies on minimum budgets, estimates that at least 38 million Americans are now living in poverty. The Department of Labor estimated that a single person living alone in a city needed a weekly income of about $45–$60 (at 1960 prices) to provide a "modest but adequate" budget. Three-person city families needed from $85 to $120 per week, while larger families naturally required even higher minimum incomes. Keyserling concludes conservatively that single persons with weekly incomes of $40 or less and multiple-person families with $75 or less do not manage even a "modest but adequate" livelihood. In 1961, 36 per cent of all single persons and 23 per cent of all families were below these income levels, poor, not in some relative sense, but actually in want.

The poor are not just the sick, the misfits, the aged, and the "rejects" of a working society. They are not just the long-term unemployed of the depressed areas or the rural poor. They are a large fraction of the working population. Although the average wage in manufacturing is now just above $100 per week, millions of workers earn far less. In April, 1963,

* Leon Keyserling, *Poverty and Deprivation in the U.S.* (April, 1962).

there were 2,180,000 production and nonsupervisory workers in textile mills, apparel manufacturing, and the leather industry whose average weekly earnings were $67, $59, and $62, respectively. The 6,319,000 nonsupervisory employees in retail stores earned an average of $67 per week. The 365,-000 workers in laundries and dry cleaning plants were paid only $52 per week, and the 542,000 employed in hotels, tourist courts, motels were paid even less—an average $47 per week. None of these wages can adequately support a family, and the lowest wages in the service trades are barely enough to sustain a single person above the level of bedrock needs.

Even more troubling, progress in reducing the number of poor families has slowed down to a snail's pace in recent years. In the ten years from the middle of the great depression to 1947, the number of poor families (with weekly incomes equivalent to $75 or less in 1960 prices) declined from 21 million to less than 14 million. This was a reduction of family poverty at the rate of 4.8 per cent per year. From 1947 to 1953, the number of such families was further reduced to 11 million—at a rate of 2.7 per cent per year. But in the seven years from 1953 to 1960, reduction in family poverty proceeded at a rate little more than 1 per cent per year. Poor families still numbered 10 million in 1960.*

If progress in eliminating poverty has been so slow and

---

* Leon Keyserling, *Taxes and the Public Interest,* Conference on Economic Progress (June, 1963), p. 26. The rich, on the other hand, have been getting richer. A study of wealth ownership by Professor Robert J. Lampman of the University of Wisconsin reveals that the fortunes of the very rich in the period after 1953 followed a course just the opposite of the poor. In the decade 1939–49, increased employment and incomes for the poor, and high taxes levied on the rich, reduced the share in the nation's wealth of the richest 1 per cent of the population from 30.6 per cent to 20.8 per cent. But from 1949 onward, the richest 1 per cent gradually increased its ownership of wealth to 24.2 per cent in 1953, 26 per cent in 1956, and 28 per cent in 1961.

there are so many poor people in this country, why have we had to be reawakened to these facts? How did 40-odd million people manage to become "invisible"? *

There are three main reasons.

First, the proportion of the poor in the population has declined drastically since the years of the great depression. In those years unemployment, poverty, and despair struck deep into the ranks of the middle and upper classes. Keyserling estimates that in 1935–36, more than two-thirds of all American families were poor—President Roosevelt's dramatic image of "one-third of a nation" was, in fact, a vast understatement of the breadth of poverty at that time. When professional men were selling apples on Wall Street and the formerly well-to-do appeared in the bread lines, it took no effort of the imagination to see poverty as a national problem. But as the ranks of the poor thinned out, those who were able to leave poverty behind also left behind their feeling of kinship with the poor. A few years of financial security and prospects for personal advancement and one no longer thought on meeting a poor person "There, but for the grace of God, go I."

Second, there has been a massive increase in the numbers enjoying comfort and affluence. According to the Department of Commerce † 23 per cent of all consumer units—families and individuals—had personal incomes in 1962 of between $8,000 and $15,000, and another 7 per cent had incomes above $15,000. In 1929, only 8 per cent of all American families and individuals were in these two upper income groups. The affluent 30 per cent of the population have been able to look at each other and, as Dwight McDonald said in a recent

---

* This is not to suggest of course that the problem of poverty has not continued to concern scholars and government officials. The Joint Economic Committee, for example, has published at least ten studies of the problem in recent years.

† U.S. Department of Commerce, "Size Distribution of Income in 1962," *Survey of Current Business*, April, 1963, p. 15.

article, assume that they *are* the nation.* They are so many, and there are no poor among them.

Third, the comfortable and affluent have been assisted in their illusion of the disappearance of poverty by moving away from it. While the poor have remained in the miserable housing of our urban slums, the middle and upper classes have moved to the suburbs. The breadwinner's daily trip back and forth to the office or the suburban family's occasional forays into town take place by rapid transit or over superhighways. It is hard to see the masses of poor people jammed into slums and tenements within the central cities.

RISE IN UNEMPLOYMENT
AND DECLINE IN GROWTH OF EMPLOYMENT †

It is not to minimize the problem of poverty or the shame of its existence in a rich country to say that the problem of high and rising unemployment is, in a fundamental sense, the more serious. Much of the problem of poverty arises from causes outside the operation of our economic system. But the problem of unemployment derives directly from the system itself.

It is true that many poor people are poor because they work at ill-paid jobs or have no jobs at all. But many others are thrust into poverty by physical or mental disability, illness, the death of the breadwinner, or incapacitating old age. We can alleviate this kind of poverty through compassionate social measures, but we cannot entirely eliminate its causes.

In the case of unemployment, concern for its victims would be an inadequate response—the causes for most of it can be eradicated. To be complacent in the face of helpless poverty

* Dwight McDonald, "The Invisible Poor," *The New Yorker,* Jan. 19, 1963, p. 96.

† All of the figures on United States employment and unemployment in this and following sections of the chapter are taken from Department of Labor sources, particularly from *A Report on Manpower Requirements, Resources, Utilization, and Training,* March, 1963, referred to in the text as Department of Labor Manpower Study.

is to be lacking in heart. To be complacent in the face of rising unemployment is to be weak in the head.

The facts of unemployment are sharp and clear.

In successive peak prosperity periods since 1953, the overall rate of unemployment in this country has risen—from 2.9 per cent in 1953; to 4.3 per cent in 1956–57; to 5.6 per cent in 1959–60; and to between 5.5 and 6 per cent in 1963.

In July, 1963, 4,322,000 people, 5.6 per cent of the civilian labor force, were officially counted as unemployed. In addition, another 924,000 people were working in part-time jobs only because full-time jobs were not available. The full-time equivalent of their partial unemployment is about 1.2 per cent. Thus, the true rate of unemployment is today nearly 7 per cent.

The present high level of unemployment in this country contrasts very unfavorably with the record of other leading industrial countries. A study by the Department of Labor, in which foreign unemployment data were carefully adjusted to reflect United States definitions of unemployment, showed that in 1960 our unemployment rate of 5.6 per cent was exceeded only by Canada's 7 per cent. In the same year, unemployment was 4.3 per cent in Italy, 2.4 per cent in Britain, 1.9 per cent in France, 1.5 per cent in Sweden (1961), 1.1 per cent in Japan, and 1 per cent in Germany.* Three per cent is a reasonable goal for the United States, conservative both in terms of our 1953 2.9 per cent, and in terms of the rates in other industrialized countries.

While unemployment has been going up, growth in employment has been slackening. In the ten years 1947–57, nonfarm wage and salary jobs grew at the rate of about 900,000 per year. But from 1957 to 1962, only about 480,000 nonfarm wage and salary jobs were added each year. In both periods, farm jobs declined at the rate of about 200,000 per year.

From 1947–57, every major category of nonfarm employ-

---

* U.S. Department of Labor, "International Comparisons of Unemployment," *Monthly Labor Review,* August, 1962, p. 863.

ment, except mining, grew. After 1957, in all but one major category of employment, there was either an absolute decline in the number of jobs or a decline in the rate of increase. As shown in the table below, only state and local employment (largely school teachers) showed a higher rate of employment growth after 1957 than before.

	Average annual percentage growth or decline in employment	
	1947–57	*1957–62*
Mining	−1.4	−4.8
Manufacturing	+1.0	−0.5
Contract construction	+4.0	−1.6
Transportation, public utilities	+0.2	−1.5
Trade	+2.0	+1.2
Finance—insurance—real estate	+3.5	+2.4
Services and miscellaneous	+3.0	+2.8
Federal government	+1.6	+1.1
State and local government	+4.2	+4.8

The fact that unemployment has risen to high levels since 1957 is not surprising in view of the general decline in jobs added throughout the economy. It is often assumed that employment in services is expanding rapidly but it should be noted that in two service fields—construction, and transportation and public utilities—there were actual job losses after 1957 instead of increases. In two other service fields, trade and finance-insurance-real estate, the rate of new jobs created dropped sizeably.

THE HUMAN COSTS OF UNEMPLOYMENT

To say that people need jobs in order to eat and to provide for other immediate needs is to miss most of the truth. In our work-dominated society, a job earns full membership in the "club," respect in the eyes of others, and self-respect. This is so nearly universally true for men of working age that those with independent means who deliberately choose to be idle are regarded with more than a little suspicion.

A job gives hope for material and social advancement. It is a way for providing one's children a better start in life. It may mean the only honorable way of escape from the poverty of one's parents. It helps to overcome racial and other social barriers. In short, for most men and an increasing number of women of working age, a job is the passport to freedom and to a better life. To deprive people of jobs is to read them out of our society.

Moreover, the curse of unemployment lies nearly as heavily on the children of the unemployed as on the victims themselves. If parents cannot work, their children are deprived of normal education and medical care. They are often subjected to a demoralized home atmosphere.

Yet it is sometimes suggested that instead of trying to provide jobs for the unemployed, we ought to pension them off in some way. Such a "solution" is morally repugnant and socially dangerous. But even as an economic matter, the proposal is absurd. Is it really sound policy to start paying a pension from early youth to old age to an able-bodied person, rather than to find that person a place in our economic life? Those who have jobs are not likely to consent to the indefinite payment of unemployment compensation to millions of able-bodied people.

We have only to remember what provision we now make for the aged, to whom we acknowledge a debt, under a contributory system started nearly three decades ago. The average monthly benefit for a retired worker under Federal Social Security is now only some $76 per month, not much more than $900 a year. Were we to provide equally inadequate unemployment compensation to 4 million unemployed, there would be an annual cost approaching $4 billion—a cost which would grow as unemployment increased.

Not all unemployment is bad. Some of it is voluntary—as people take time off after leaving one job before looking seriously for another, or as they leave a job in one place to take a different or better job in another. Some of it is involuntary but of relatively short duration. Moreover, in some occupations seasonal unemployment is inevitable—construction workers in Northern cities, summer stock actors, employees in fruit and vegetable canning. But 3 per cent of the work force is the most generous conceivable allowance for "frictional" unemployment.

The burden of unemployment falls particularly heavily on two large groups in our society—Negroes and young people.

Negroes. Negroes account for only 11 per cent of the labor force, but for 22 per cent of the unemployed. In every age group, in every occupational classification, and in every industry Negroes have much higher rates of unemployment than white workers—frequently as much as three times as high. In 1962, when the over-all rate of unemployment was 5.6 per cent, white and Negro rates of unemployment were as follows:

	White	Negro
Over-all rate	*4.9*	*11.0*
Boys, 14 to 19 years	12.3	20.7
Men, 25 years and over	3.6	9.4
Clerical workers	3.8	7.1
Craftsmen and foremen	4.8	9.7
Factory production workers	6.9	12.0
Private household workers	3.1	7.1
Professional and technical workers	2.0	3.5

Moreover, jobs for Negroes have been available in volume only in the lower-paying unskilled farm and nonfarm occupations, semiskilled factory occupations, or in the service trades. In the professions and technical occupations, Negroes are clustered at the less-skilled, less-rewarded end of the occupational range.

High unemployment combines with low pay to give the Negroes as a group an economic status which the country as a whole has not known since the Thirties. In 1960, only 20 per cent of all Negro families had incomes of $6,000 or more, while nearly half of all white families were in this class. More than 60 per cent of all Negro families and individuals were poor (family income of less than $75 per week; individual income of less than $40 per week). About 28 per cent of white families and single individuals were in this submerged economic class.

The economic problem of our Negroes is more than unemployment alone. It is a problem of pervasive discrimination in jobs, housing, education, political rights, public accommodations—the entire front on which the civil rights battle is raging today. But high unemployment and, particularly, disproportionately high unemployment, is a basic cause of their just indignation. If Negroes had more and better jobs, they could justifiably feel that they had taken a meaningful step out of a vicious circle toward full-scale membership in American society.

Young People. The general rise in unemployment and the decline in job opportunities have meant a much higher than average rate of unemployment for young people. In 1962, when the over-all unemployment rate was 5.6 per cent, young men of 18 and 19 had an unemployment rate of 13.8 per cent, while those aged 20–24 had a rate of 8.9 per cent.

It is, of course, to be expected that unemployment would be higher for young people than for older, more experienced, more settled people. Many are just entering the labor force and have yet to acquire training and higher skills. They also change jobs frequently in the search for an opening which promises the maximum chance for advancement in the future.

Only in times of abounding job opportunities can the unemployment rate for young people be kept down to the minimum.

For example, in the years 1950–52, young men of 18–19 had unemployment rates varying from 6.6 to 6.8 per cent instead of the 13.8 per cent of 1962. Those aged 20–24 had unemployment rates ranging from 3.5 to 4.3 per cent instead of the 8.9 per cent of 1962.

If today's situation is serious for young people, the next few years could be calamitous for them. We are just entering the period when the children born during the post-World War II baby boom are reaching maturity and entering the labor market. Compared to the relatively small numbers of youth who entered the labor market in the past decade, we face an onrush of tidal-wave proportions in the demand for jobs by this group.

During the Fifties the number of workers under 25 increased only from 13,330,000 to 13,700,000. In the 1960's this age group will increase by over 6 million. By 1970, the economy will have to provide 20 million jobs just for people under 25.

If this huge need is not adequately met and young people are not given their due in job opportunities, the human and social consequences for this country are incalculable. Massive disillusionment among the young at a time when they need the greatest inducement to continue education and to work hard acquiring skills could create a truly revolutionary situation. Delinquency and crime rates would rise, and extreme political movements could flourish. Whatever the directions in which protest or revolt take place, our society would be an unbecoming one of entrenched maturity closing the doors to its own children.

THE ECONOMIC COSTS OF UNEMPLOYMENT

Loss of output. In prosperous Western Europe, labor is a precious resource. Europe's rapid rate of economic growth required not only full use of their own labor, but millions of foreign workers. After the vast immigration from Eastern

Germany ceased, Western Germany turned to Italy and Greece for more workers. France has welcomed laborers from Tunisia, Morocco, and Algeria. Switzerland relies heavily on neighboring countries for an added labor supply.

The United States, far from having to bring in manpower, has not been able to use what it has. Our failure to employ our own labor force means an enormous waste of potential production.

What does this annual waste amount to?

Let us look at the number of added workers involved in a reduction of the unemployment rate to 3 per cent. Some 1,850,000 persons now recorded as unemployed would be employed if the present unemployment rate were reduced to 3 per cent. Another 750,000 persons, according to the Department of Labor's estimate, could be added to the employed if persons involuntarily in part-time jobs could have the full-time jobs they seek. An additional 900,000 persons * who are not now counted among the unemployed because they are discouraged from actively seeking work by the scarcity of jobs, could be added to the employed if the economy had enough zip to provide the new jobs for the partially and completely unemployed groups. Together, these amount to some 3.5 million persons.

How much added output would these additional 3.5 million workers produce? Increased output per added worker for the year July, 1962–June, 1963, a period of relatively stable economic activity, was $17,000. Increased output per added worker for the year January, 1962–December, 1962, a period of more rapidly expanding economic activity, was $26,000.

If we take the low figure of output per added worker—

* Chairman Walter W. Heller of the Council of Economic Advisers estimated the number at 800,000–1,000,000 in testimony before the Joint Economic Committee, Hearing on the Economic Report of the President, January, 1963, p. 59.

$17,000—the output of the additional 3.5 million persons would be $60 billion. If we take the high figure of $26,000 the additional output would be $90 billion. And this $60–$90 billion estimate will increase as the number of potential workers, most of them young, increases.

These calculations of loss of output assume that the 3.5 million persons added to the employed are roughly as productive as those added to the work force in the 1962–63 periods used. In an actual reemployment program, the increased output per added worker would be lower, particularly if the program were rapid. This is so because efficiency would decrease as full employment was approached.

On the other hand, the calculations may well be on the conservative side because they fail to take into account the many workers now wastefully employed at low-productivity occupations. A million or more Americans now working on marginal farms could more productively be employed in a fully employed economy. And eliminating job discrimination against Negroes and other minority groups, and thus increasing their productivity by utilizing their best skills, has been estimated by the Council of Economic Advisers as sufficient by itself to increase annual output by $13 billion.

The Council of Economic Advisers has been using a much lower figure as its estimate of what our waste of manpower costs this country in output—something around $30 billion a year.* This estimate is explained by the Council's use of 4 per cent as an unemployment goal rather than 3 per cent, and by its failure to take into account the types of underemployment mentioned above.

James W. Knowles, executive director of the Joint Economic Committee, made an extensive study in 1959 of loss of

* Gardiner Ackley, Member, Council of Economic Advisers, Address to Western Economic Association, San Francisco State College, August 22, 1963.

output. He estimates that at mid-1963 underutilization of our resources cost us about $40–$45 billion of lost output. Again, this estimate assumes an unemployment goal of 4 per cent.*

These losses—at least $30–$60 billion—are losses we can ill afford. With a higher level of output, we could raise the standard of living of the 40-odd million people now submerged in poverty. Although more food would not be required for this purpose, more of nearly everything else would—from clothing, housing, and medical services to a share in the luxuries most of us take for granted.

Moreover, as Prof. Paul McCracken of the University of Michigan recently told a meeting of the American Bankers Association, we need to remember that the income of the typical family in this country is still around $120 per week—of which roughly $25 must be paid in taxes. As McCracken emphasized, "it should strain no one's imagination to believe that this average American family could produce quite a long list of very commendable items that it would like to buy if there were a little more of this thing darkly referred to by some as private affluence." †

Added output means a higher share for everyone of public goods and services which the Federal, state, and local governments must supply—from slum clearance, cleaner air, safer drinking water, better street and highway systems to recreational facilities, playgrounds, and parks.

Added output, too, means that we will be better able to help developing countries, both through trade and aid, as discussed in Chapter 4.

* James W. Knowles, Study Paper No. 20. "The Potential Economic Growth of the United States" (January, 1960) (prepared in connection with the Joint Economic Committee's study of Employment, Growth, and Price Levels). Estimate for 1963 supplied by Mr. Knowles, using the formula worked out in Study Paper No. 20.

† American Bankers Association, *Proceedings of a Symposium on Economic Growth,* February 25, 1963, p. 24.

Loss to workers, employers, and the state. Persistently high unemployment means higher costs for workers, employers, and the state.

As unemployment rises and unemployment compensation funds are exhausted, pressures increase on employers and the Federal government to increase contributions. Governments at all levels are confronted with the need to supply more public assistance. As juvenile delinquency and crime rates increase, business and personal losses due to pilferage and property damage go up, and law enforcement costs rise. More ambulances, more firefighting equipment, and more jails become necessary.

When unemployment forces older people into premature retirement, the cost to workers and employers of maintaining even an inadequate pension system will rise. The social security pension costs will in any case rise as the proportion of the aged in the population rises and life expectancy lengthens. If in addition we force people to retire before they want to, and while they are still able to work efficiently, an additional cost will needlessly be imposed on the younger people in the labor force.

When unemployment is high, those who have jobs may lose their investment in education and in time spent to acquire higher skills. The woman with a graduate degree is used as a typist; the skilled technician is demoted to a production job; the production man is pushed into a laborer's job; and the laborer becomes another statistic among the unemployed. Business organizations which were perfectly prepared to hire and to train high school graduates in a variety of jobs suddenly start demanding college graduates. Where a B.A. degree once sufficed, now higher degrees and more specialized training are required.

Loss from "job-saving" practices. The employed 94 per cent of our labor force are far from feeling secure as they see the creeping advance of unemployment. To the extent that they are able to do so, they will try to save their jobs. Many of these attempts are costly for the economy.

Skilled workers in the construction trades, for example, try to restrict entry into their fields. In New York City, protests of Negro groups have publicized the attempts of craft unions to limit apprenticeship programs to the sons and nephews of present members. Such practices, of course, increase the cost of construction when a building boom is on. But the workers tend not to be interested in higher productivity and lower costs because their boom-and-bust experience has taught them that jobs suddenly disappear, whatever they do.

Other workers show their insecurity by resisting technological advance—not by smashing machines but by other forms of resistance. A principal issue at stake in the months-long New York newspaper shutdown was the objection by the printers to the use of prepared advertising mats and automatic printing machinery. Railroad firemen object to being laid off even though they are not needed to fire diesel locomotives. The airline flight engineers took issue with the airlines on whether their presence in planes was essential. In each of these cases, the job-saving attempts are understandable, but they inevitably increase costs to employers.

Where enlightened employers and unions work together, management may be able to introduce cost- and laborsaving methods without the opposition of labor. This has happened in the 1963 arrangement between the Kaiser Steel Company and the United Steel Workers, in which part of management's cost savings is devoted to retraining employees, and part to a bonus to the workers.

If unemployment continues to rise, general increases in unit costs of output may occur, because the work week may have to be reduced in order to share out available job opportunities. The leadership of the AFL-CIO has warned that unless measures are taken to reduce the present high rate of unemployment, it will open a drive for a 35-hour week without any reduction in pay or other benefits. We have already seen a variant of this proposal in the contract negotiated between the steel workers and their industry, where it was agreed that workers would receive much longer paid vacations.

Now, there is nothing sacred about the 40-hour week or the present agreements with respect to length of vacations. Indeed, increases in productivity should be channeled at least partly toward such increased leisure. A 35-hour week by 1970 is a realizable goal. But abrupt and major reductions in work-hours could bring about disturbing rises in unit costs. This could in turn cause distress to some businesses. To the extent that it increased prices, exports, in particular, would suffer. Thus, a major reduction in the work week as a means of meeting the immediate problem of unemployment presents serious difficulties. On the other hand, a heavy responsibility rests on policy makers to come up with a good alternative, since we cannot continue to place the burden of unemployment on the back of a minority of the labor force.

High unemployment: demand or "structural"?

Is the gradual rise in unemployment in successive periods of prosperity since the Fifties due mainly to inadequate demand? If it is, the principal remedy is to increase over-all demand, by some combination of easier money, taxing less, or spending more. As increased demand causes employers to increase their output, they will themselves find and train people to take over new jobs. Publicly supported programs for educating and re-training people, improving employment services, and helping people to relocate, will be merely a supplement.

The opposite view is that held by the "structuralists." They assert that our chronic unemployment is mainly caused not by a serious inadequacy of demand, but by built-in "structural" factors.* Because of these "structural" factors, they argue, large increases in over-all demand would simply result in inflation. In its extreme form, the "structuralist" argument almost denies that unemployment exists: our only trouble is that workers cannot or will not accept the abundant opportunities for work!

The "structuralists" point to the present rate of automation and technological advance as eliminating jobs—particularly unskilled ones—much faster than formerly. They point to the shift in demand from blue-collar factory jobs to white-collar jobs in factories and services. They point to what they say is a lessened willingness by workers to change their occupations or to move to areas of labor demand.

This basic question—whether the major cause of our unemployment is lack of over-all demand or "structural"—has to be answered. If the cause is lack of demand, general stimulation of the economy is the main remedy; if the cause is "structural," retraining, educating, and helping people to relocate must be the main remedy.

I conclude that insufficient demand is the main cause of our unemployment, and that creating sufficient demand must be the main remedy. Automation does not seem to be moving appreciably faster than earlier technological advances; even if it should prove to be moving faster, the principal means of providing jobs for those displaced by the machine is still expanded demand. There are a few jobs now going begging because blue-collar workers lack training facilities to become white-collar workers, or because unemployed workers in a particular area or industry cannot or will not move to areas where there are jobs. But all the training, area redevelopment programs, and mobility aids in the world will not compensate

* For a statement of the "structural" view, see testimony of Federal Reserve Board Chairman William McChesney Martin, before the Joint Economic Committee, *Hearings,* February, March, and April, 1961, pp. 470–473.

for an over-all lack of demand. How can you have on-the-job training if there is no job?

Let us now take a detailed look at each of the three main categories of "structural" unemployment.

AUTOMATION AND TECHNOLOGICAL CHANGE

Has technological advance recently speeded up, with a resulting higher displacement of workers? The instinctive answer is "yes." The mind leaps to machines which can guide other machines—computers and electronic guidance systems which appear in a magical way to instruct other machines, which in turn do the work. No one can fail to be impressed by the way a computer analyzes cost and market-demand factors to "find" the best balance of output for a petroleum refinery—a balance automatically communicated to other machines which complete the production process. Machines can now tell management how much of what materials to order for inventory. They can pick up delicate components in proper order for final assembly into complicated wholes or adjust traffic light systems in major cities to changing traffic conditions throughout the day.

Yet the great leaps forward in the technology of the past were at least as impressive. The harnessing of steam as motive power for ocean vessels displaced the great sailing ships. The steam locomotive and the motor car made the horse technologically unemployed. Diesels later replaced steam engines on railroads. Mechanical conveyor belts replaced the pick-up-and-carry systems in mining and manufacturing. Giant excavating and earthmoving equipment replaced shovels and wheel barrows. Dial telephones and automatic exchanges have taken the place of manually operated telephone systems.

Moreover, more efficient organization of production and factory layout, without adding machines or workers, has increased output throughout the modern industrial period. Frederick Taylor, who revolutionized factory systems, made his contribution in the early years of the century. Recently production engineers have learned to inject oxygen into open hearth furnaces, greatly increasing the output of steel within a given time period.

Because of the variety of ways in which more output can be obtained with a given unit of labor, no measures are available of the progress in automation or technological change as such. Instead we have figures on increases in man-hour productivity brought about by all causes.

These figures show that the most recent rates of increase in man-hour productivity for the economy as a whole, while somewhat above the average for the past 50 years, are no higher than the average for the entire postwar period. The average annual increase in productivity for the years 1957–62 was 3 per cent, the same as the average for the period 1947–62, as opposed to 2.4 per cent for the entire period 1909–62.

Furthermore, productivity has frequently increased at a much higher rate than the 1957–62 average of 3 per cent. In 1948–53, for example, it increased at the rate of 4.3 per cent. Actually, after a spurt in the 1948–53 period following World War II, technological change and all other factors contributing to man-hour productivity have in fact slowed down instead of speeding up.

Moreover, in the 1948–53 period, unemployment fell from 3.8 to 2.9 per cent. In 1957–62, when productivity rose at a slower rate, unemployment went up from 4.3 to 5.6 per cent. Thus the higher rate of productivity increase in the earlier period was accompanied by an *improved* unemployment rate, rather than the *worsened* rate that one would expect if increased productivity inevitably caused unemployment.

SHIFT FROM BLUE-COLLAR
TO WHITE-COLLAR OCCUPATIONS

The "structuralists" reason that another cause of our recent high unemployment is that blue-collar, as contrasted with white-collar, workers are being displaced at a higher rate than at earlier times. Now it is perfectly true that there has been a continuing shift from blue-collar to white-collar jobs within manufacturing, as well as a shift in the labor force from manufacturing to services. It is also true that unemployment rates for blue-collar occupations, particularly for unskilled workers, are today far higher than for the labor force as a whole.

What is not true, however, is that there has been any marked *increase* in the blue-collar unemployment rate today over some earlier period. Neither has there been any marked *decrease* in the white-collar unemployment rate today over some earlier period.

A study made by the Joint Economic Committee in 1961 * showed that blue-collar unemployment rates in recent years are not larger, relative to the over-all rate of unemployment, than in earlier years. According to the study, factory production workers and nonfarm laborers have always suffered disproportionately in times of high unemployment, and there is a generally consistent relationship between their rates of unemployment and the over-all rate of unemployment. For example, the unemployment rate of factory production workers in 1960 had about the same relationship to the over-all unemployment rate at it had in 1949. The unemployment rate of nonfarm laborers has been about twice as high as the over-all rate in recent years, but this was also about the relationship in earlier years.

On the other side of the picture, the committee found that, while white-collar workers have in recent years had lower unemployment rates relative to over-all unemployment than blue-collar workers, the same was true in earlier years. By and large, unemployment among sales workers, clerical workers, and even professional and technical employees went up when general unemployment rose and declined when the over-all

* Joint Economic Committee, *Higher Unemployment Rates, 1957–60: Structural Transformation or Demand,* 1957–60, November, 1961.

rate fell, though not as much as among blue-collar workers.

If unemployment rates for blue-collar occupations have tended to rise faster recently than those for white-collar occupations, as the "structuralists" contend, the proportion of blue-collar workers among the unemployed would also have risen. As the following table shows, this is not the case:

	Per cent distribution of unemployed	
	1953	*1962*
Total	100.0	100.0
WHITE-COLLAR GROUPS	20.5	21.4
Professional, technical, and kindred workers	3.0	3.5
Managers, officials, and proprietors	3.8	2.8
Clerical and kindred workers	8.5	10.4
Sales workers	5.2	4.7
BLUE-COLLAR GROUPS	70.8	62.4
Craftsmen, foremen, and kindred workers	14.5	11.5
Operators and kindred workers	26.5	24.3
Private household workers	3.0	3.0
Service workers, other than private household	12.0	11.1
Nonfarm laborers	14.8	12.5
FARM GROUPS	4.4	2.8
Farmers and farm managers	.6	.2
Farm laborers and foremen	3.8	2.6
NO PREVIOUS WORK EXPERIENCE	4.4	13.4

Indeed blue-collar workers were a *lower* proportion of the unemployed in 1962, when over-all unemployment was high, than in 1953, when the rate of unemployment was very low. Another fact brought out by the table is that the percentage of those who had no previous work experience—mostly young people—more than trebled between the two periods. Their increase among the numbers unemployed is certainly not due to the type of skills they bring to the labor market, but to a general decline in employment opportunities.

If there had been an unusual shift in demand from blue-collar to white-collar occupations, there would be widespread shortages in many white-collar occupations. While comprehensive figures on job vacancies are not available, the March, 1963, Department of Labor Manpower Study * shows that labor shortages today are mainly those in certain professional occupations requiring long years of education and training, or those requiring special skills.

Professional job vacancies exist for certain types of engineers, mathematicians, physicists, astronomers, metallurgists, oceanographers, meteorologists, biochemists, biophysicists, microbiologists, pharmacologists, doctors, dentists, psychologists with advanced training, social workers, economists, social scientists with advanced training, college professors with Ph.D degrees, and high school teachers of mathematics, science, and foreign languages.

There is also demand, usually local, for skilled technicians in many engineering and physical-science specialties, elementary school teachers and teachers of the industrial arts, good stenographers, well-trained office workers who can type, chefs, tailors, practical nurses, hospital attendants, automobile mechanics, TV and radio repairmen, and servicemen for appliances, business machines, and air-conditioning equipment.

Suppose we educated, trained, motivated, and transported people to wherever all these jobs are (incidentally, this is what we should be doing to the best of our ability, whether it be producing a Ph.D. in microbiology by years of graduate work, or an auto mechanic by a short vocational course). At most, this would enable a few scores of thousands of job seekers to fill job vacancies. Compare this with our 4.3 million unemployed, and with the 1.5 million job seekers who will be com-

* U.S. Department of Labor, *Manpower Report, op. cit.*

ing into the labor market every year from now on, and the more than a million displaced every year by automation. Obviously our high unemployment cannot be explained away as due simply to an unusual demand for white-collar workers at the expense of blue-collar workers.

Perhaps the most far-fetched "structural" argument of all is this one: "Unemployment cannot much be reduced, because we will immediately run into terrible production bottlenecks due to the shortage of high-level personnel, and thus increased demand will only cause inflation." This argument is largely nonsense. In industrial plant after industrial plant, there are skilled workers qualified to be made foremen; foremen ready to be advanced to plant superintendent; plant superintendents capable of being general manager. That the nation has a shortage of astronomers does not mean that our factories and our construction crews are not capable, here and now, of tremendous increases in production.

LABOR MOBILITY

Few people in modern times have been as willing to pick up and move as Americans. While war, persecution, and famine have caused vast migrations among other peoples, Americans have moved since the early colonial days in response to new opportunity. And the 1960 Census confirms that this is still going on.

Of the 159 million persons 5 years old and over in 1960, 28 million had moved from one county to another in the same state, or from one state to another, within the last five years.

Between 1950 and 1960, four out of every five counties in the United States, many of them rural, lost population because of emigration. The one out of every five which gained residents through immigration was nearly always an urban or suburban county, or benefited from the immense shift from agricultural into nonagricultural occupations.

In general, the states and regions which had net gains were

those which had employment increases; the greater the number of jobs added, the greater the number of new people attracted to the area. The Pacific states, the Eastern seaboard south of New England, the Mountain states, and the Southwest showed both large increases in employment since 1955 and a large migrant population in residence in 1960.

The states that lost the most population (averaging over 400,000 each) were Pennsylvania, West Virginia, Mississippi, Arkansas, and Kentucky. Three of these states—Pennsylvania, West Virginia, and Kentucky—contain depressed coal mining areas from which people fled. Mississippi and Arkansas, as well as other states of the South, lost population as poor white people from rural areas and Negroes moved to areas of greater job opportunity.

Considering the size and character of recent population shifts, the American's traditional willingness to move when jobs can be found has not changed in the least. A thoughtless reaction to depressed areas and rural slums is "So why don't people move?" The answer is that they have—in millions. And still more would move if there were jobs to move to.

Nonetheless, it is sometimes contended that the growth of private pension plans has decreased labor mobility. No studies have ever been made of the extent to which this may be true. About 23 million workers, roughly half of all private nonfarm workers, are now covered by pension plans. Nearly all plans pay benefits only after a worker has been covered for periods ranging from 10 to 20 years.

Therefore pension plans are likely to affect only those workers with substantial seniority. Among those with seniority, restraints on mobility have been reduced for some 10 million workers by vesting, early retirement, and portability rights. Even among those whose plans do not contain such rights, mobility of many is not likely to be seriously retarded, because of the very small benefits payable. Most covered workers would have to earn an average of $4,800 per year for 20 years to be entitled to pensions ranging from $10 to $60 per month.

Thus "structural" changes play a very minor role in our present unemployment. The 1961 Joint Economic Committee Study concluded that, at most, "structural" factors may be contributing a few tenths of a per cent to our present high unemployment rate. Though we should do everything possible to retrain workers and to help them find new jobs, the main problem is to increase demand in the economy.

Is the deficiency in consumption or in investment?

To increase demand so as to utilize our present idle resources of manpower and industrial capacity and permit the economy to operate at a higher rate of sustained growth, we must determine the kind of demand which the economy now lacks.

Various kinds of demand for final products, added together, give us the nation's gross national product for a given period. In the year 1962, our gross national product of $555 billion was composed of consumers' expenditures of $355 billion; private domestic investment (including housing), $79 billion; government expenditures (Federal, state and local), $117 billion; and net exports, $4 billion.

Obviously a boost in demand big enough to affect the total must come from a change in one of the first three categories, since net exports are not of significant size in relation to the total. Although all three categories are significant, the first two—private consumption and private investment—are together the most important in determining the level of total economic activity. Whatever we determine the level of government expenditures should be, the total of private consumption and private investment must grow if the economy is to grow.

Since the economy's continued growth is dependent on

maintaining an adequate productive capacity, a fundamental question is whether private investment should be stimulated directly, or whether increased investment should come as a result of efforts to boost the level of consumer demand.

KENNEDY ADMINISTRATION:
EMPHASIS ON INVESTMENT

The Kennedy Administration chose first the alternative of direct stimulation of business investment. The reasoning was that consumers' expenditures could be depended upon to maintain a fairly steady upward growth, but that business investment behaved erratically and had recently not kept up with the growth of the economy. In 1960, plant and equipment expenditures came to about $36 billion, less than the amount which had been invested in 1957 when the economy had been smaller.

Thus President Kennedy said in his economic message to Congress of Feb. 2, 1961, a few days after his inaugural

. . . Both full recovery and economic growth require expansion of expenditures for business plant and equipment, for state and local governmental facilities, and for residential construction. . . .

The President recommended special tax incentives for investment, saying that

. . . an early stimulus to business investment will promote recovery and increase employment.

Steps were taken to revise depreciation rules so that business could write off equipment investment more rapidly. A tax credit of 7 per cent on new investment was enacted. Both were effective for the entire year of 1962. Together they added $2.3 billion to corporation cash reserves, an amount equivalent to a reduction in 1962 corporate taxes by 9 per cent.* As a

* U.S. Department of Commerce, *Survey of Current Business,* July, 1963, pp. 3–9.

result, corporate internal cash reserves available for investment increased from $29.6 billion in 1961 to $34.9 billion in 1962.

As a further inducement to investment, the Federal Reserve System attempted to prevent an increase in long-term interest rates by a combined policy of maintaining an ample supply of reserves in the banking system and of direct purchases of long-term United States government securities for its own portfolio. Long-term interest rates, therefore, declined a bit during 1962, but they failed to come down to levels which in former years were regarded as necessary for stimulating new investment. The main difficulty was that the Administration and the Federal Reserve were simultaneously attempting to hold up short-term interest rates for balance-of-payments reasons. However, despite the generally high level of interest rates, business sentiment agreed that the cost of money was not a major impediment to investment.

Unhappily, business capital spending refused to increase appreciably. Expenditures in 1962 for plant and equipment totaled $37 billion, 9 per cent more than in 1961, but not much more than the amount invested in 1957.

The Joint Economic Committee had warned in its 1961 annual report that efforts to stimulate business investment might fail:

Additional investment is desirable because it can raise productivity and lower costs. If these lower costs are translated into lower prices, consumers can be benefited and total demand for goods and services can be expected to increase. However, the principal inducement to expansion of capital must be the prospect of increased demand for products which capital produces. It may be that a tax incentive to a faster rate of investment will have relatively little stimulus to investment unless final consumer demand is stimulated. . . .*

* Joint Economic Committee Report on the January 1961 Economic Report of the President, pp. 34–35.

In November, 1962, Secretary Dillon in a statement to the President's Advisory Committee on Labor-Management Policy conceded that the strategy of directly stimulating investment had failed:

We had hoped, a year ago, that with this added stimulus the economic recovery would carry us to full employment by the end of the current fiscal year [1963]. Unfortunately, the economy has failed to expand as rapidly as we had hoped and expected. . . .*

In 1963, the Administration shifted its emphasis to give more weight to the expansion of consumer demand. The program envisaged tax reductions of about $9 billion for individuals. While it thus conceded something to the commonsense view that investment is not going to increase while excess capacity abounds, it by no means abandoned the view that direct stimulation of investment was necessary, and included a further reduction of about $2 billion in the corporation income tax.

The Joint Economic Committee's 1963 Report emphasized the need for prompt action on the tax reduction program. It recommended that most of the reductions take place in 1963, and that the tax savings be given largely to individuals in the lower income brackets. The committee also recommended the reduction or elimination of excise taxes which had been enacted at a time when it had been necessary to curtail consumer demand.

Some critics of the Administration program were not so kind. In an editorial entitled "The Right Remedy but Late and Little," the editors of *Business Week* said:

. . . the President's program must be regarded with mixed feelings. The country needs a massive tax cut. It needs such a cut promptly, without the delay and confusion that inevitably will re-

* Conference of President's Advisory Committee on Labor-Management Policy, Nov. 14 and 15, 1962.

sult from the ill-advised attempt to cancel out part of it under the name of loophole closing.

Clearly, the Administration is on the right track at last. But its program is still too narrow in scope, too slow in timing, and too complex in detail to be what the country needs.*

CONSUMPTION NEEDS STIMULATION

Tax policy must concern itself with a variety of criteria—impact on the economy, yield to the Treasury, equity to the taxpayer. We are here concerned only with the first of these. The thesis that investment can be much stimulated by tax reductions to corporations and to high-bracket individual taxpayers, rather than to low- and middle-bracket individual taxpayers, disregards the fact that our main deficiency today is in consumer demand. Until consumption catches up with investment in a significant range of industries, tax reductions to corporations and to high-bracket individual taxpayers will call forth little additional capital investment.

Even after two successive years of booming automobile production, capacity in the industry is so ample that its 1963 investment was projected at only an additional $70 million in 1962, as contrasted with an additional $560 million spent in 1956 over 1955. To add significantly to automobile production facilities, a level of demand even higher than the present one of around 7 million cars per year would probably be necessary.

Every dollar of tax reduction not spent either for consumption or investment is a dollar that does not stimulate the economy. Only a vastly expanded consumer demand can remedy our present underconsumption, which is in turn responsible for the lagging rate of investment today. Low- and middle-bracket individual taxpayers are the most likely to spend the extra income, and thus provide the increased demand needed. Higher-bracket taxpayers who receive extra income

* *Business Week,* Jan. 26, 1963.

through tax reductions will save a larger proportion. This saving, like corporate saving, stimulates the economy only at times when it can be converted into new investment.

This is the central reason why unemployment can best be fought by stimulating consumption directly, and thus induce needed investment, rather than by undue emphasis on investment alone. There are additional reasons:

Lessened need for physical capital today. Dr. Raymond Goldsmith, in his 1962 testimony before the Joint Economic Committee, pointed out a basic change which has been occurring in the American economy. He believes that we now need much less capital than in earlier stages of our development for the same quantity of production. The growth in real output per capita during the years since World War II was about the same as the growth during the period 1870–1929. *But post-World War II growth has required a much smaller capital outlay.**

A study by Edward F. Denison for the Committee for Economic Development† arrives at the same conclusion.† Denison finds that in the period 1909–29, 23–26 per cent of each percentage point in the national growth rate was due to capital investment, but that in the period 1929–57 this ratio was only 15 per cent.

While the lessened need for physical capital today emerges clearly from the statistics, just why this is so is not so clear. Is it because consumer demand focuses increasingly on services, ranging from beauty parlors to psychiatry, which require relatively little physical capital? Is it because government expenditure increasingly emphasizes research and development, as opposed to goods like guns and trucks which require fac-

* Joint Economic Committee, Hearings on the Economic Report of the President (1962), p. 531.

† Edward F. Denison, *The Sources of Economic Growth in the United States and the Alternatives before Us,* Committee for Economic Development, 1962, p. 267.

tories and machine tools? Is it because of the shift of industry to the more temperate parts of the country, where huge winterized installations are unnecessary? Is it because today's more efficient machinery needs fewer replacements?

Because the share of capital investment in the rapidly growing industrial economies of Japan and Western Europe has been much higher than in the United States, many jump to the conclusion that more capital per worker will automatically lead to higher rates of growth for the United States. Both Dr. Goldsmith and Prof. Simon Kuznets of the National Bureau of Economic Research warn that capital investment ratios in these other countries have been highly irregular, and that nothing in their experience justifies the prescription of more capital expenditures for this country in order to attain higher national product.*

Adequacy of funds for investment.   Growth in capital investment is not being held back by lack of money, except for small business. Corporations now have in retained profits and depreciation reserves the highest level of internal sources of financing in history. In 1962, internal corporate reserves totaled $34.9 billion, more than enough to finance corporate investment in plant and equipment of $32 billion. A huge flow of personal savings is also available which can either be borrowed by the issuance of bonds or tapped by the issuance of stock.

It is clear from our recent history that corporations do not hesitate to borrow or to issue common stock in large volume when they believe capital investment will bring in good returns in the form of increased sales and profits. In 1957, when their internal reserves totaled $28 billion, corporations went into the market to get an extra $10.5 billion in new funds.

Therefore available funds for investment seem adequate.

* Joint Economic Committee, Hearings on the Economic Report of the President (1962), p. 532; also Kuznets, *Economic Development and Cultural Change* (July, 1961), IX, pp. 55–56.

Merely adding to corporate cash reserves or to personal savings of high-bracket individual taxpayers through increased dividends and tax cuts is not likely to stimulate extra investment.

Incentives for investors.   Considerations of equity may well require a restructuring of the tax bite on high-bracket individual taxpayers. But it is difficult to find objective evidence that high-income tax rates have deterred investors from capital investment they otherwise would have made. Corporate and individual investors commit their funds to a capital investment because they believe that they can make a future profit out of that investment. Unless they can make a profit before taxes, it matters little how deep is the tax bite. And whether business is profitable before taxes depends mainly on whether the plant and equipment is fully used, or lies idle a large part of the time. A comparison of before-tax corporate profits in 1955, a year in which industry was operating at 90 per cent of capacity, with corporate profits in 1961, a year in which industry was operating at 83 per cent of capacity, is instructive. In both years, incidentally, the same Federal tax schedules were in effect. In 1955, corporate profits before taxes were $44.9 billion. In 1961, corporate profits before taxes were $43.8 billion. Had the economy in 1961 operated at 90 per cent instead of only 83 per cent capacity, corporate profits would have been $58 billion instead of the actual $43.8 billion. *

* Estimate of Council of Economic Advisers, Joint Economic Committee, Hearings on the Economic Report of the President (1961), p. 334.

CHAPTER SIX

Maximum Employment, Production, and Purchasing Power

> The Congress declares that it is the continuing policy and responsibility of the Federal Government to promote maximum employment, production, and purchasing power.
>
> Employment Act of 1946

The clearly stated responsibility of the Federal government under the Employment Act of 1946 is to promote maximum employment. Government policies and actions which aim merely to reduce the present high rate of unemployment to a somewhat less painful level, by achieving a better balance between consumption and investment, are not enough.

The goal: an unemployment rate of 3 per cent

We have been successively lowering our sights on how much unemployment is too much. When unemployment rose from the 2.5–3 per cent levels of the prosperous 1951–53 period to 4 and 5 per cent in 1954, we knew that we were in a recession and that something had to be done to bring down the rate of unemployment. Today there is a common tendency to identify a 4 per cent rate of unemployment not with recession but with full employment. This devaluation of what constitutes full employment is a rank injustice to the hundreds of thousands able to work but unable to find it. It is a disservice to the principles of the Employment Act. We should stop lending support to the idea that a 4 per cent rate is acceptable. An unemployment rate of 3 per cent should be the minimum full-employment goal. To achieve it requires a program of well-balanced action in four major areas.

TAXATION

Federal income tax policy should be our principal instrument for reaching and maintaining full employment. The 1963 tax reduction program will come at least a year too late, and it will be far too little for what the economy needs.

The program appears to set a maximum reduction in individual taxes of about $9 billion, and a reduction in corporate taxes of some $2 billion. Because the prime problem today is lack of consumer demand, the stimulus to be expected from the reduction in corporate taxes is slight.

The maximum effect of the $9 billion reduction in individual taxes would at the very most add perhaps $18 billion to total demand over the course of a year. A dollar released by the tax cut would be partly saved but mostly spent. The spent portion becomes another person's income, to be partly saved and spent again, and so on, so that the initial added dollar of income adds another in about a year's time.*

Even this $18 billion estimated increase in output may be overoptimistic. Federal social security and state and local taxes will continue to rise and thus offset part of the $9 billion income tax cut. Moreover, state and local sales and property taxes fall heavily on lower-income persons and families, just the people who might otherwise have spent most and saved least of their tax-cut dollars. As these regressive taxes rise, the "multiplier" effect of continued spending in the economy is reduced, and national output gains less.

* See 1963 Annual Report, Joint Economic Committee.

Will this increased consumer spending stimulate considerable added investment, so that the original $9 billion becomes appreciably *more* than $18 billion?

If the economy were operating closer to capacity today, consumer dollars released by tax reductions would do just this. But we are now using about 87 per cent of our plant and equipment. A modest $18 billion increase in consumer spending—enough to increase plant use from 87 per cent to a slightly better 90 per cent—is not likely to convince investors that decisively more capital investment will be needed to take care of consumer demand.

When the economy is operating at as much below the full employment level as it is today, an increase of output in the range of $18 billion is not likely to be enough to reduce the number of totally unemployed to 3 per cent. That goal will require a larger tax cut than that now contemplated. In any event, taxes will have to be varied so that total demand will neither sag below full employment levels nor push the economy on into inflation. The tax rates appropriate for 1964 are almost certainly not those we will want a few years hence. Only by recognizing that tax levels may have to be changed from time to time can we assure continuing full employment without inflation. Congress, as guardian of the Federal tax system, must learn to make prompt adjustments in the rate structure consistent with this goal.

As an instrument of national economic policy, adequate tax reduction has the advantage of being felt quickly over a broad sector of the private economy. It has the obvious disadvantage of adding temporarily but substantially to the Federal budget deficit, and it cannot by itself meet the problems of structural unemployment, some of the poor, and the aged. Even an adequate tax-cut program would need the assistance of increased unemployment compensation for longer periods than are now provided, higher levels of public assistance for the poor who cannot work, and far more generous pensions for the aged.

MONETARY POLICY

Ready availability of credit and low interest rates make it easier and cheaper for businesses and individuals to undertake investment or investment-type expenditures. But when business and individual incomes are not expanding rapidly, there is a limit to the extent to which easy monetary policy can stimulate further spending. Borrowed money, unlike earned money, must be paid back. People do not borrow to spend unless they have reasonable prospects for paying it back, along with the interest on the loan. Hence there is a basic flaw in the reasoning of those who claim that monetary policy alone can get us to full employment.

In the case of well-established large businesses, easy money or low long-term interest rates cannot encourage investment any more than accelerated depreciation and special investment credits have thus far. The individual, insecure about his income, is not a good prospect as a home purchaser even though the mortgage rate is reasonable. Even consumer purchasers of automobiles and durable goods on credit are quick to pay off debt and not to incur new debt when things look bad.

But to deny the extreme claims for monetary policy of its proponents is not to say that we can therefore proceed to cut down on bank credit and raise interest rates when there is substantial slack in the economy. When a basic stimulus is injected into the economy by cutting taxes, readily available credit at reasonable cost is absolutely essential to keep the stimulus going. This is particularly true in the areas of housing construction, small-business financing, and consumer purchases of big durable items like automobiles and some types of appliances.

A chart on housing construction looks like the reversal of

a chart on long-term interest rates. When interest rates were falling in 1953 and 1954, housing starts moved steadily upward. As money was tightened and interest rates rose in 1955, 1956, and 1957, housing starts nosed downward. Again, when rates came down in 1958, housing starts rose. But they dropped quickly and stayed down as the Federal Reserve slammed on the credit brakes in late 1958 and kept them on during 1959 and 1960. Only in 1961, when mortgage rates began to decline, did housing starts again increase. The present $20-billion annual contribution of housing to the nation's output could quickly decline if mortgage rates are again raised.

Small business is particularly disadvantaged by tight money. As a study conducted by the University of Wisconsin* shows, small business is very dependent on bank credit for financing growth as well as for current operations. When bank reserves decline, bankers begin to ration credit and to make loans to the bigger, better established, more "credit-worthy" firms. Small firms, particularly new small firms, are the first to be refused loans. They suffer most, since they usually have no alternative sources of financing. The loss of output of small firms is particularly serious for the economy, for they are often the innovators and the leaders in industries of future expansion. Today, for example, small companies are notable in such new areas as electronics, automation equipment, and missile components.

Despite the need for an easy monetary policy and a steady increase in the money supply to encourage growth, the Federal Reserve has consistently favored tighter money than a full-employment goal requires. Since 1955, the annual growth in our money supply (currency and demand deposits) has averaged less than 1½ per cent, less than one-half the 3 per cent average of the last century. While the Fed has felt obliged to ease up on the credit brakes for short periods during

---

* University of Wisconsin, *Attitudes of Wisconsin Bankers toward Small Business Financing,* September, 1961.

acknowledged recessions, its eagerness to use the brakes has led it to justify tightening at all other times for a variety of ill-assorted reasons.

In October, 1958, when the economy was barely recovering from a severe recession, the Federal Reserve saw inflation looming. It reported:

Expectations of renewed inflation are at least as widespread today as they were in the early summer of 1957. They constitute the major current threat to the continued progress of our recovery.*

When the inflation argument began to sound silly in the face of stable prices, the balance of payments was trotted out as a reason for tightening credit. Recently, in 1963, not satisfied with a drastic curtailment of free reserves in the banking system and an increase in the rediscount rate from 3 to 3½ per cent—for balance-of-payments reasons—Federal Reserve Chairman William McChesney Martin, Jr., started a campaign to persuade lenders not to be so willing to lend. He testified that "credit quality has deteriorated," as lenders have sought to make loans to borrowers they could not have accommodated when money conditions were tighter.†

Unfortunately, the propensity of Chairman Martin to regard tight money as the proper condition to which the rest of the economy must somehow adjust has received support from some who surely should know better. The Council of Economic Advisers, for example, in its 1963 report accepts the balance-of-payments arguments for higher interest rates:

. . . defense of the currency may require vigorous use of monetary instruments, and there can be no doubt that the U.S. authorities are prepared to take whatever steps are necessary to defend the dollar.‡

* Letter of Federal Reserve Board staff included in study by Asher Achinstein, *Federal Reserve Policy and Economic Stability, 1951–57,* Senate Committee on Banking and Currency, 1958.

† House Banking and Currency Committee Hearings, July, 1963.

‡ Annual Report of the Council of Economic Advisers, January, 1963, p. 59.

Although this statement makes it sound as though the Administration were trying to force tight money on a reluctant Chairman Martin, the situation recalls the dying Kentucky Colonel who summoned his wife to his bedside for a last request:

My dear, fetch my old silver goblet, fill it with ice from the spring-house and mint from the herb-garden. Pour over it the 1895 Bourbon in the iron safe in my study. Wait until the frost forms on the outside of the cup. Then, put it on my bed-table—*and, no matter what I say, make me drink it.*

Even conservative economists have voiced their protests against the tight-money policies of the Federal Reserve.

Dr. Arthur Burns of Columbia University, and chairman of the Council of Economic Advisers under the Eisenhower Administration, said in a 1961 address at the University of Chicago:

Many factors undoubtedly contributed to the unsatisfactory character of the business-cycle expansion from 1958 to 1960, but I believe that three developments were decisive.

First of all, we had a violent shift in Federal finances. . . .

Second, the fiscal restraint on general economic expansion was accompanied—indeed preceded—by a tightening of credit conditions.

By mid-1959 commercial banks were already in debt at the Federal Reserve to the tune of $1 billion. The money supply stopped growing. Demand deposits diminished by nearly $4 billion between July 1959 and May 1960. Interest rates rose sharply, both on short-term and long-term loans. Indeed, long-term rates advanced faster than during a comparable stage of any business cycle during the past hundred years. . . .*

Dr. W. Allen Wallis, dean of the University of Chicago Graduate School of Business and formerly economic adviser to Vice-President Nixon, told a 1961 gathering of business

* *Congressional Record,* Apr. 27, 1961, pp. A2886–A2887.

executives that the Federal Reserve Board tightened up the money supply in 1959 "over-vigorously and over-promptly" as a move against inflation. Wallis said that the inflation against which the Fed was acting "wasn't there." *

Walter Fackler, associate dean of the Graduate School of Business, University of Chicago, formerly of the U.S. Chamber of Commerce, says in a recent article:

. . . For the past year, we have followed an essentially deflationary monetary policy, and I predict that we will suffer sad consequences therefrom. We have sacrificed the domestic interests of the country on an altar of gold and allowed the deficit in our international balance of payments to override all other policy considerations. From my reading of the Washington temper, it seems likely that we will continue to depress the economy and keep unemployment high in an attempt to protect our gold stocks by ill-advised methods. I certainly cannot be accused of being an "inflationist," and I am fully aware of the complex set of problems posed by our international economic position. But neither am I a "deflationist," and I gravely fear that the "deflationists," with their fear of nonexistent inflationary pressures and their sloganeering about a "sound dollar," have won the day—and have put us in a most unfortunate policy bind. The fact is that an economy can no more be run without money than a car can be run without gasoline. We have set the monetary carburetor on the economy so lean that it simply cannot generate sufficient power to move forward. And no amount of talk or fancy footwork by the Treasury in the bond market will get it moving again.†

It is sometimes concluded that because Western Europe and Japan have achieved prosperity and rapid economic growth with a higher level of interest rates than in the United States, tight money and a slow growth in the money supply would not hurt this country. Two things are wrong with this assumption. First, Europe's relatively high interest rates today

* Milwaukee *Journal,* May 10, 1061.
† Walter D. Fackler, "Business Spending and Government Fiscal Policy," *Journal of Business,* University of Chicago, January, 1963, pp. 2–3.

ANNUAL INCREASES IN GROSS NATIONAL PRODUCT AND MONEY SUPPLY (1955 equals 100)

Country	1955	1956	1957	1958	1959	1960	1961	Compound annual percentage increase
			Gross National Product					
Japan	100	110	124	122	147	171	210	13.18
France	100	110	124	141	152	168	181	10.40
Germany	100	110	120	128	139	158	174	9.68
Italy	100	108	116	124	132	144	159	8.03
Switzerland	100	107	113	118	124	134	148	6.75
United Kingdom	100	109	115	120	125	132	140	5.77
Canada	100	113	118	121	128	132	136	5.27
United States	100	105	111	112	121	127	130	4.47
			Money Supply					
Japan	100	116	121	137	159	190	226	14.56
Italy	100	108	115	127	144	164	191	11.39
Germany	100	107	120	136	152	162	186	10.90
France	100	110	120	127	141	160	185	10.80
Switzerland	100	107	110	122	128	141	163	8.48
Canada	100	99	103	116	112	118	133	4.87
United Kingdom	100	101	104	107	112	111	113	2.05
United States	100	101	100	105	105	104	109	1.45

* House Banking and Currency Committee, *Hearings*, July, 1963, p. 39.

were still higher in an earlier period—they have been coming down, particularly in the last few years. Second, their present level of interest rates exists because of booming growth and despite very large annual additions to the money supply. As the preceding table which I submitted to the House Banking and Currency Committee during its July, 1963, hearings shows, the higher the rate of growth of the country, the larger was the average annual addition to the money supply. The United States' rate of growth, and of additions to the money supply, are both at the bottom of the list.

A full-employment program in this country cannot be achieved without a monetary policy which assures a steady supply of credit at reasonable rates of interest. As pointed out in Chapter 3, safeguards against capital outflow to foreign countries should in the main be sought in a better international monetary mechanism, leaving to monetary policy the unhampered task of attending to the needs of the domestic full-employment program.

PUBLIC EXPENDITURES

Public expenditures—Federal, state, or local—should be dictated by those needs which only governments can provide. Heavy reliance on public spending to make up for large deficiencies in over-all demand in the economy is undesirable for several reasons. It can lead to unwise, wasteful expenditure. If used to prime the economy, public works expenditures are slower and less widely distributed in their effects both industrially and regionally. Conversely, when total demand starts to exceed the full-employment level, necessary cutbacks in public spending are likely to be too slow, too little, and too drastic in their effects on particular industries and areas. And, most important, a frequent large-scale intrusion into and subsequent withdrawal of the government from the economy could be seriously unsettling to the enterprise system.

For a good long-term program of public expenditures we

must achieve better Federal-state-local understanding of how to divide responsibility for essential public services. National defense and the space program are clearly the jobs of the Federal government; police and sanitation are mostly local problems. But in between are a number of critical areas where joint activity is necessary:

Education. In the Sixties, the group aged 5–19 years will increase by 10 million. An enormous expenditure for additional buildings and for competent teachers will be required for all educational levels from kindergarten to graduate schools. In this critical area, it will take the combined efforts of the entire community—private as well as public—to meet the needs. It will take financial support from local, state, and Federal sources.

Failure to provide adequately for education will not only deprive the next generation of the intellectual heritage to which it is entitled. It will prevent adding to the most important form of capital for the future growth of the country. The education of the labor force is a far greater element in increased productivity than the land, buildings, and machinery which we normally regard as constituting capital. As Prof. Theodore W. Schultz of the University of Chicago told the American Economic Association in December, 1960:

Although it is obvious that people acquire useful skills and knowledge, it is not obvious that these skills and knowledge are a form of capital, that this capital is in substantial part a product of deliberate investment, that it has grown in Western societies at a much faster rate than conventional (nonhuman) capital, and that its growth may well be the most distinctive feature of the economic system.

It has been widely observed that increases in national output have been large compared with the increases of land, man-hours, and physical reproducible capital. Investment in human capital is probably the major explanation for the difference.

Much of what we call consumption constitutes investment in human capital. Direct expenditures on education, health and internal migration to take advantage of better job opportunities are clear examples.

Health and welfare.   Both compassion and the desire to protect communities from the blight of poverty and sickness require that we make far more generous provision for those who need public assistance—the aged, the blind, the disabled, the sick, families with dependent children, and others who have no other sources of support. The amounts which combined Federal-state programs now provide are inadequate. For example, in December, 1962, the average monthly payment to an aged person on relief was $75. The average per recipient in families with dependent children was $31. As a minimum, we should have a comprehensive system of medical care for the aged under the social security program, so that the costly hazards of illness do not impose the humiliations of public medical assistance on aged persons and huge additional costs on the public authorities.

Urban renewal and transit.   Despite substantial progress in urban renewal, we have barely begun the massive job of rehabilitating the central cities in our growing urban areas. Much more public housing is needed for those uprooted by slum clearance and expressways. Failure to do so in the past has not only imposed great hardship on those dislocated, but has caused the deterioration of other areas into slums. The explosive problem of urban mass transit has followed in the wake of city growth and the abandonment of existing public transit systems in favor of the automobile. The coordinated action of Federal and city governments is urgently required to prevent the throttling of economic life by traffic tieups.

Conservation and agriculture.   The accumulating problems of conservation (maintaining adequate supplies of pure water and keeping air free from industrial and radioactive pollution; providing parks and recreation areas and preserving fast-disappearing wildlife and wilderness) are enormous areas of continuing responsibility for Federal and local governments alike.

In addition, the Federal government must reconsider its basic policies in agriculture. A depression-born system of agricultural subsidies, intended to prevent gross injustice to a major sector of the economy, is now the source for billions of dollars of income transfers from the rest of the nation to thriving industrial-scale farms. But it benefits the millions of marginal farmers very little. While continued agricultural supports have helped to build the most productive agriculture the world has ever known, it is time to confront some fundamental facts. About half of our present 3.7 million farms now produce over 90 per cent of the nation's total output of food and fiber. With the huge advances in productivity characteristic of our agriculture, this half of our farms could more than provide for our continuing domestic and international food and fiber requirements.

Federal funds ostensibly to support "family farms," but actually largely devoted to increasing profits for large commercial farmers, would be better used for converting suitable areas vacated by agriculture to recreation grounds where all citizens could enjoy some of the values traditionally associated with the family farm; and for assisting the people from nearly 2 million farms to move to more productive activity in non-farm occupations. Apart from our unemployed, agriculture provides the largest unused reservoir of labor power for economic growth which we now have.

This rational redirection of our efforts in conservation and agriculture would require a major reorganization of both the executive and legislative branches of the Federal government. The entrenched interests represented by our Department of Agriculture and the agricultural committees of the Congress should give way to a Department of Conservation and Congressional conservation committees.

Culture. Granted that the basic material needs of our people must take precedence in the concern of governments for the public welfare, Federal, state, and local government—operating usually through private institutions, universities, and foundations—should give substantial support to cultural activities and the construction of cultural centers throughout the United States. The postwar rebuilding of many European cities stands as both a reproach and a shining example to far wealthier American cities. I saw Stuttgart, Germany, as a mass of rubble in World War II. The next time I saw Stuttgart was in 1962. The Federal, state, and local governments had combined to build a hundred schools, a great university, an opera house, theaters, symphony and chamber-music halls. We must resolve to do the same for the downtown areas of our own cities. Unless we do, no amount of rebuilding and renewal will give them the life which distinguishes a city from a mere agglomeration of buildings.

A "work-and-learn" program. As we have seen, the "structural" problems of unemployment—the inability of the economy to absorb blue-collar workers, the unskilled, inexperienced youth, and people in depressed rural and urban areas— are largely those of inadequate demand. If this demand were forthcoming, the problems of "structural" unemployment could largely be solved by the private economy. Both in the World War II and Korean War periods, private employers were able to absorb huge numbers both of the urban unemployed and of untrained workers from rural poverty. The employers provided the training and retraining needed.

Nevertheless, both because the present tax-cut program is likely to prove inadequate and because of the huge backlog of people who require training and retraining, it will be necessary for the Federal, state, and local governments to expand present manpower training and depressed areas programs. But training accomplishes little if there are no jobs for those being trained. And it is no encouragement for the jobless to be told that three or four years hence added demand may create jobs for them. The immediate problem of the unemployed is that they need jobs, and they need them *now*.

I have suggested a "work-and-learn" program under which Federal grants would be made to local communities or non-profit institutions such as hospitals for worthwhile local projects. The program would aim at finding useful interim jobs for many thousands of long-time unemployed who have exhausted their unemployment compensation, and of young people who cannot find their first job.

The job would consist partly in work on a project, partly in going to school—either job training at a vocational school, or learning to read and write at a continuation school. Thus the program would come to grips with our grave social problems of disillusion and discrimination by providing self-respect through immediate work, and a new skill, even if it be only the gift of literacy, for the future. In the relatively rare case of someone needing no training, there could be just the job.

The weekly wage for the hours of work and study would be sufficient for a minimum standard of living, though obviously somewhat lower than the prevailing wage in the locality. Eligibility would depend upon "working and learning" in good faith.

The local community or nonprofit institution would be required to do its part. It would have to meet the non-labor costs, and to supply supervision. Projects would be those with a high labor intensity, such as modifying the land for a new recreation area near a metropolitan center, or helping in a neighborhood or downtown "clean-up" campaign supervised by the city or by an organization such as the Urban League.

In order to receive support, a project would have to be established as additional to anything that would be undertaken without the work-and-learn program.

Since the work-and-learn program would not involve large-scale public works, it could get under way as soon as enacted. Unlike large-scale public works programs, it could be phased down and discontinued just as rapidly as the over-all economy provided more durable jobs.

Military, space, and research expenditures. About two-thirds of the entire 1963 Federal budget was spent on the defense, space, and research programs of the Federal government. The great bulk of these funds have been concentrated in the Pacific, Southwest, and Eastern seaboard states, which explains in large part the more rapid growth of these areas over the past decade. Far greater thought will have to be given to the allocation of these funds, particularly for research, so that basically well-endowed areas like the Midwest are not stripped of resources for future growth.

The obviously great impact of Federal military and space spending not only on certain geographic areas but on the economy as a whole means that the sudden withdrawal of this demand would have the gravest consequences. With partial disarmament again within the realm of political possibility, we should lose no time in considering specific tax, expenditure, and retraining programs which will be needed when defense expenditures can be cut back.

Foreign aid. Just as raising the incomes of poor Americans is part and parcel of the problem of our national growth, assistance in raising the incomes of poorer countries is an indispensable part of the building of the free world community. This task, too often thought of as an unpleasant whim of Washington bureaucrats, is in fact the joint responsibility of all Americans who constitute, as a group, the richest nation in the world. With the growth in our national output, particularly as we succeed in attaining a full-employment rate of growth, we can well afford to give or to lend a larger amount of our production as an investment in the wider community, as discussed in Chapter 4.

ANTI-INFLATIONARY MECHANISMS

An unbalanced Federal budget during an advance to full employment will not pose a threat of general-demand inflation. With full employment, the budget will balance or produce a surplus with which to retire debt. If demand is not sufficiently curtailed by the size of the surplus when we reach full employment, tax increases will be necessary in order to avoid inflation.

In the process of moving toward full employment, there is another kind of inflation which may occur—administered price increases in strategic industries through the interaction of powerful industries and powerful unions. It was this type of inflation which the Federal Reserve System tried to combat with tight money in 1955–57. Tight money did nothing to cure administered-price inflation; it only brought on a recession.

Administered-price inflation is less likely today than in that earlier period. There is now wider understanding of the far-ranging effects which price increases in basic materials like steel can have on the entire economy. Increased competition from both imports and domestic substitutes will continue to moderate inflation in the administered-price industries.

The Council of Economic Advisers made a substantial contribution in their 1962 annual report by recommending guidelines for wage and price increases. In addition, a procedure such as that proposed in a bill introduced by Sen. Joseph Clark of Pennsylvania and myself in 1959 may be needed. Under that bill, public hearings would be held by a board composed of public, industry, and labor representatives on wage or price increases in major industries before they were negotiated or made effective, so as to bring an informed public opinion to bear on decisions in which the public has a vital stake.

One is led to the reluctant conclusion that the Federal government is defaulting upon the responsibility to promote maximum employment imposed on it by the Employment Act of 1946.

Our blight of unemployment and poverty in the midst of general affluence is getting worse, not better. If we let it worsen, we let a major solvent for the problem of racial discrimination—jobs for all—slip through our fingers.

The Federal government is defaulting on its maximum-employment responsibility, as we have seen, largely because the arithmetic of our taxation and expenditure policies is wholly inadequate to bring unemployment down to a tolerable level, and to enlarge national income and government revenues to the point where the budget can be balanced. And the present trend of monetary policy portends an additional drag upon the economy.

The half-hearted approach to full employment stems mainly from the Administration's fears of what it assumes to be the political realities. Any larger tax cuts than those proposed, the Administration argues, will result in larger immediate budget deficits, greater than those in the Eisenhower period.

But the trouble here, as has been pointed out, is that the present program will not do the job. It will not measurably decrease unemployment or generate a national income sufficient to balance the budget. The political consequence, therefore, is likely to be to discredit in the public eye the enlarging of demand as the way to deal with unemployment. We shall then be prey to any Know-Nothing movement that plumps for an immediate balanced budget at a low level of growth and a high level of unemployment. The ensuing recession is one that we cannot afford from either the domestic or the international standpoint.

Fiscal policy, like skiing, requires a certain amount of daring. In skiing, if you attempt to negotiate a turn too slowly and cautiously, you don't get around at all. Only when you throw yourself bravely down the mountain does the turn work.

The same principle applies to fiscal policy. The economy is not going to make the required turn if the attempt is timid and half-hearted. Only by a meaningful increase in demand, principally through an adequate tax cut with supporting monetary and expenditure policies, can there be an upsurge in consumption sufficient to stimulate investment and thus produce a total demand which will achieve our goal of 3 per cent unemployment, and with it a national income sufficient to yield the revenues to balance the budget.

CHAPTER SEVEN

Political Flesh on the Economic Bones

> The question now is whether the peoples of the countries which are still free are capable of attaining, by the paths of liberty and of the spirit, a sufficient moral unanimity.
>
> Jacques Maritain

We look back upon the 1930's as a nightmare of economic nationalism. Great swings in the economic cycle produced depression and mass unemployment throughout the Western world. Countries attempted to "export their unemployment" by building up export surpluses at somebody else's expense. The system of international payments collapsed. World trade, such as it was, came to be carried on more and more by bilateral barter deals.

The free world has come a long way from the Thirties. But economic nationalism has by no means vanished.

Examples are plentiful. In 1962 the United States raised its tariff on glass and carpets, two prominent Belgian exports. The Common Market promptly retaliated by raising its tariffs on our polyethylene plastic, practically cutting off our exports. When Canada in late 1962 raised its rediscount rate to 7 per cent in order to help its international-payments position, it caused embarrassment for the United States by attracting our short-term capital movements to Canada. Many of the countries of Western Europe have rigid quotas discriminating against Japanese imports.

If the countries of the free world are to move toward the kind of community in trade, payments, aid, and growth which this book advocates, they first have to agree on what needs to be done.

Here a central problem presents itself. Heads of state worry about alliances and nuclear testing and diplomatic recognition and other noneconomic matters. Economic matters, on the other hand, tend to be delegated to specialists—central bankers and finance ministers, trade experts and aid technicians.

How can this tendency to handle international economic problems on a compartmentalized and often technical basis be reversed?

A tempting solution, always, is a summit conference on the subject by the free world heads of state. But there are two difficulties here. Summit conferences are necessarily infrequent in nature, and the problems of international economics move too fast to wait for them. More importantly, summit conferences are the voice of national interests alone: there tends to be no one speaking for the common interest of the community.

A continuing institution is needed to handle the business of building a free world community. Lord Franks, former British Ambassador to the United States, put the problem very well recently:

. . . the partnership of the Atlantic group of nations cannot get where it wants simply by the established processes of cooperation and negotiation: conferences with the unanimity rule and the compromising urgency of the problems no longer permit it. A new way has to be found: a new organization, institution or commission, which will have sufficient standing, independence and initiative to formulate common solutions and put them forward to the governments of the several nations of the group, so that they will have to face in argument not merely each other but also and at the same time the solution proposed for the partnership as a whole as best realizing its common good.*

Fortunately no new organization is required. We need not begin with a blank sheet of paper. There is already in being an organization that lends itself to further development in order "to formulate common solutions."

This is the Organization for Economic Cooperation and Development (OECD), which came into existence on Sept. 30, 1961. It has the right membership and the right areas of activity. But it must be built up in prestige and structure to become the forum for conducting the free world's business. Three devices that have served West Germany, France, Italy, and the Benelux countries in building their integration of Europe can provide new strength to the OECD.

The OECD's members are the United States, Canada, France, Germany, Belgium, the Netherlands, Luxembourg, Italy, the United Kingdom, Sweden, Norway, Denmark, Portugal, Austria, Switzerland, Ireland, Iceland, Greece, Turkey, and Spain. Japan, long associated with the OECD as a member of its Development Assistance Committee, has now been received into full membership. Yugoslavia and Finland have observer status. With a little leeway of definition in one or two cases, and if Australia and New Zealand are added, these comprise the developed countries of the free world.

The OECD is proving a workable forum for joint action by its members in the vital fields of world trade, aid for developing areas, strengthening the international monetary system, and promoting policies designed to foster in each country maximum employment, economic growth, and price stability. A list of OECD's eight permanent committees well indicates the breadth of its international interests: scientific affairs, economics, trade and payments, development, manpower and social affairs, industry, agriculture, and nuclear energy.

* *Foreign Affairs,* October, 1962, p. 33.

Indeed, the business of OECD is about as broad as the business of the free world, with the single exception of military affairs, which are deliberately excepted from OECD's charter because the organization includes neutrals such as Austria, Sweden, and Switzerland.

But the OECD, though it is concerned with the free world's vital interests, and though its membership comes close to the list of the free world's industrialized nations, now lacks the "standing, independence, and initiative to formulate lasting solutions."

While it has a secretary-general, there is no real executive agency. No one is charged with initiating policies. Its council, consisting of one representative of each member country, has only occasional meetings filled by ministers, rather than lower-level meetings filled by permanent representatives. And it lacks any legislative body or consultative assembly.

How can the OECD be given sufficient "standing, independence, and initiative" so that it can play a major role in formulating common solutions to the free world's problems of trade, aid, payments, and growth?

It is within the realm of political feasibility to bring this about by drawing on several devices which have worked successfully in the integration of the Six of Europe. The three communities which constitute the political framework of the Six, the European Coal and Steel Community (ECSC), the European Economic Community (EEC), and the European Atomic Energy Community (Euratom), employ four main institutions. Two of them, the European Parliament and the Court of Justice, are common to the three communities.

Councils of ministers, technically distinct for each community but actually composed of the same officials, represent the member countries and make final decisions on the measures which member nations must take.

The two commissions of the EEC and Euratom and the

High Authority of the ECSC, in addition to carrying out the work of their communities, have the power and duty of making proposals for the Six as a whole.

The Parliamentary Assembly has the power to debate the affairs of the communities and to force the resignation of the executives by votes of censure carried by a two-thirds majority. This power has not yet been exercised, but the parliament has on several occasions used its threat of censure to bring about a particular action by the commission.

The executive and legislative instruments of the Six could be adapted to the OECD in the following ways:

The OECD Council could be given vastly increased standing if it were elevated to a Council of Ministers, and if in each member country the relevant minister were given cabinet rank. Needed, too, would be a determination on the part of OECD members that they would conduct their foreign economic policies mainly through OECD. As at present, any country could reject the application to it of an OECD decision. Incidentally, some genius at nomenclature might be assigned the task of thinking up a more inspiring title for the organization.

Thought should also be given to a device like the EEC Commission for the OECD. A commission of, say, five distinguished members, picked from nationals of the member countries for a fairly long period of office by the Council of Ministers, would have standing. With members of international stature—a Paul Hoffman, a Lord Franks, a Jean Monnet—the Commission's recommendations would carry great weight. If it recommended that the member countries should erect a proposed new international monetary mechanism, or should adopt more coordinated policies on aid, or should work toward more rational domestic agricultural policies, the Council of Ministers would be less disposed to whittle the recommendations down to what would satisfy the most difficult member. The members of OECD could readily create such a commission by their joint agreement.

A third move to strengthen the OECD could perhaps be brought about even before the other two. This is the proposal for the creation of an OECD Parliamentary Conference. Such a conference was proposed by OECD Secretary-General Thorkil Kristansen in June, 1962.

An OECD Parliamentary Conference could consist of around 100 delegates, roughly proportioned to the populations of the 20 member countries, with at least one delegate for each country. At least initially, delegates should all be legislators, selected by their own legislative bodies. But they would vote according to their own consciences, rather than by country or bloc.

The Parliamentary Conference could be empowered to debate everything within OECD's competence; to pass resolutions for the OECD Council and the OECD Commission; to obtain information and reports from the OECD.

Part of the value of an OECD Parliamentary Conference would be educational. It could educate the public in member countries by introducing public debate, now absent from OECD deliberations. It could educate members of the various legislatures to think about international problems in terms of their effects in all the member countries.

To participate in formulating OECD policies would be particularly important to United States Congressmen. While the cabinet members who attend official OECD meetings from Europe and Canada are almost all members of their nations' legislatures, our delegates are not. Yet programs which the OECD may formulate are highly likely to require ultimate approval by the United States Congress—whether the program is a tax cut to accelerate growth, recommended tariff-cutting legislation, an international-payments agreement, or long-term arrangements for sharing international aid. A parliamentary conference would enable members of Congress, in the late Senator Vandenberg's phrase, to participate in the takeoff as well as in the crash landing.

How could such an OECD Parliamentary Conference be

brought into being? It could easily evolve from an existing parliamentary group, the Consultative Assembly of the Council of Europe. The formation of the OECD group could lead to the elimination of this assembly and at least two of the other eight major existing interparliamentary groups, thus lessening the multiplicity of international parliamentary organizations.*

* Besides the Consultative Assembly of the Council of Europe, existing interparliamentary groups include: (1) The Interparliamentary Union, founded in 1889, with a current membership of 69 nations from both sides of the Iron Curtain. It meets annually in the capital of one of its members. The United States group is theoretically composed of all members of Congress, but delegates are restricted by law to 18, 9 each from the Senate and the House. The IPU is represented on the United Nations Economic and Social Council and has a Pan-American Branch that meets biennially. The organization's aim is to further better relations among nations through study of international law and organization, reduction of armaments, economic problems, intercultural relations, social questions, and representative government. (2) The Nordic Council, founded in 1953, with 53 parliamentary representatives from Norway, Sweden, Denmark, and Finland. (3) The Western European Union Assembly, founded in 1954, with 89 delegates from the seven-country Western European Union, consisting of Belgium, the Netherlands, Luxembourg, France, Italy, Germany, and the United Kingdom. Its orientation is largely defense and it is now practically superseded by NATO and the Council of Europe. (4) The NATO Parliamentarians Conference, founded in 1955, with 180 delegates from the fifteen-member NATO—Belgium, the Netherlands, Luxembourg, France, Italy, Germany, the United Kingdom, Denmark, Greece, Iceland, Norway, Turkey, Portugal, the United States, and Canada. This is the only group of parliamentarians acting on an Atlantic basis. It was first suggested in 1954 by Norwegian and Canadian parliamentarians in order to get NATO action in the economic field. The creation of the OECD in 1961 has tended to supersede most of NATO's economic jurisdiction. It meets annually in Paris. Its regular working committees give an idea of its range of interest—political, military, scientific and technical, economic, and information. It is quasi-official, meeting at the invitation of the NATO Secretariat, and without formal status. The Atlantic Convention of the fifteen NATO nations, an unofficial group of private citizens, in the "Declaration of Paris," January 1962, recommended that the NATO Parliamentarians Conference be developed into a consultative "Atlantic Assembly." The NATO Parliamentarians Conference, on November 16, 1962, asked its political committee to study the proposal. (5) The Benelux Consultative Parliamentary Council, founded in 1957 with 49 delegates from the Benelux Customs Union. (6) The European Parliamentary Assembly of the European Coal and Steel

The Council of Europe, founded in 1949, has 16 member countries which—together with the United States, Canada, Spain, Portugal, and Japan—make up the membership of the OECD.* Its Consultative Assembly has become a forum for debating European questions and obtaining governmental action on agreed conclusions. Its 135 members are appointed by their national parliaments, rather than directly elected, and meet once a year at Strasbourg, France, for not more than a month.

A two-thirds majority of members present may make recommendations to the Council's Committee of Ministers or to member countries. Debate has covered all matters of common interest other than national defense. The assembly has proposed conventions, which have generally been ratified by the member countries, on human rights, social security, patents, coordination of university requirements, extradition, movement of persons, blood bank exchange, television programs, and refugee visas.

Three times, on Apr. 29, 1960, on March 3, 1961, and again on Sept. 25, 1962, the Consultative Assembly has recommended that it become the parliamentary arm of the OECD by measures to tie in the OECD members not now represented in the Assembly.

Community, the European Economic Community, and the European Atomic Energy Community. It has 142 delegates from the six members of the three Communities, and although its members are now named by the national parliaments, proposals for direct election are under consideration. (7) Canada-United States Interparliamentary Group, founded in 1959, with half of its United States membership of 24 from the Senate and half from the House. It meets annually. (8) The Mexico–United States Interparliamentary Group, founded in 1960, with a United States membership of 24 divided between the House and the Senate. It meets annually. In addition, the United States sends legislative observers each year to meetings of the British Commonwealth Association of Parliamentarians, and United States Congressmen have met with British, French, and West German parliamentarians separately.

* Spain is associated with the Council of Europe for cultural purposes.

On Feb. 1, 1962, the Consultative Assembly and the OECD agreed that the present 16-member assembly would debate OECD business, with the OECD to cooperate by replying to questions presented by the assembly. By resolution of Jan. 17, 1963, the assembly appointed a delegation empowered to:

Approach the Committee of Ministers and the Governments of member states in order to persuade these Governments to enter into negotiations with the United States and Canadian Governments with a view to carrying into effect the arrangements proposed by the Assembly; and to establish later, if necessary, direct contacts with the American Congress and the Canadian Parliament with a view to contributing to the conclusion of an agreement and to its practical application.

Besides the Consultative Assembly, the Council of Europe has a Committee of Ministers, but this institution has not achieved much significance.

As it stands, the OECD is hampered by the lack of a parliamentary assembly. The Consultative Assembly, for its part, is limited by its primarily European membership and the lack of a real executive. The remedy suggests itself. The OECD Council should accept the suggestion of the Consultative Assembly that, enlarged by the addition of the OECD countries not now members, it constitute an OECD Parliamentary Conference.*

This would make the continuation of the NATO Parliamentarians Conference unnecessary, except if NATO believed a Parliamentarians Conference to discuss purely military affairs not within OECD's competence was justified. If NATO felt so, the 15 NATO members could readily provide that their delegations to the OECD Parliamentary Conference constitute themselves NATO parliamentarians for debate on military affairs after the OECD Parliamentary Conference had adjourned.

A further opportunity for avoiding duplication appears in the Canada–United States Interparliamentary Group. This was

* A Concurrent Resolution to express the sense of Congress as favoring this development (H. Con. Res. 87) was introduced by me on Feb. 7, 1963.

set up in 1959 because there was then no interparliamentary group such as the proposed OECD Parliamentary Conference. The necessity of the Canada–United States Interparliamentary Group could be reviewed if such an OECD Parliamentary Conference were created.

Thus as many as three existing parliamentary organizations —the Council of Europe's Consultative Assembly, the NATO Parliamentarians Conference, and the Canada–United States Interparliamentary Group—could be consolidated into one OECD Parliamentary Conference.

The remaining interparliamentary groups would still have their own reasons for continuing their existence.

An invigorated OECD, though it consisted of the advanced nations only, would be in no sense a "rich man's club." Its main reason for being would be to provide an environment in which the poorer nations may prosper.

These developing nations would be encouraged to create and nourish their own regional organizations to act as "opposite numbers" to the OECD. The Organization of American States, the Central American Common Market, and the Organization of African Unity are already in being for Latin America and Africa. Asian federal organization comes a little harder, but there are possibilities, provided current hostilities are overcome, in a future Pan-Malayan federation (Malaysia, Indonesia, the Philippines), and a Mekong River grouping (Viet Nam, Cambodia, Laos, Thailand, perhaps Burma). Community in the Middle East, though urgently necessary, will come harder still.

The analogy to the Marshall Plan days is clear. There the United States Economic Cooperation Administration provided the aid and (for a while) the advice, while the Committee for European Economic Cooperation and later the Organization for European Economic Cooperation divided up the aid and the burden of cooperating.

From our standpoint, there would be no constitutional objection to an invigorated OECD. The present rule that council decisions do not apply to a dissenting member would continue. But a pair of voices that tend to transcend mere national interests—the commission and the parliamentary conference —would insure that no country would lightly disregard a proposed common solution for a common problem.

One word more about international organizations. For the kinds of free world cooperation which seem possible now, the structural changes suggested for the OECD appear adequate. But if the East-West struggle became more relaxed, if the split world showed signs of coming together, if world disarmament approached reality, a supranational agency much stronger than the present United Nations would obviously be needed. Disarmament is impossible except with a world institution capable of keeping international law and order. A revitalized United Nations would have to supervise disarmament in every country; it would have to maintain a police force capable of enforcing international order; it would have to enact a considerable body of world law, including an enforceable system for protecting human rights everywhere on the globe.

But the fact that so much more may be needed one day should not delay us in setting about doing that which we can do now. No more constructive political step could be taken than for President Johnson to ask the other OECD heads of state to meet at the next OECD meeting, there to upgrade the Council of Ministers, create an OECD Commission and a Parliamentary Conference, and to undertake liaison with the evolving regional groupings of the developing world.

Turning from procedure to substance, the heads of state could then lay the groundwork for a new round of multilateral free world-wide tariff-cutting, for a new international monetary mechanism, for an advanced-nations' aid program of the dimensions needed, and for an understanding of the need for growth and full employment everywhere.

CHAPTER EIGHT

Making Congress Effective

"I can call spirits from the vasty deep."

Glendower

"Why, so can I, or so can any man; but will they come when you do call for them?"   Hotspur

Shakespeare, *Henry IV*, Part I: Act 3, Scene 1

The proposal to build a free world community based on trade, aid, a sound system of payments, and full employment is one that logically extends much of what the late President Kennedy worked toward. In this chapter we shall assess the chances that the American people will respond to effective leadership with a "general will" for such a free world community. The real question is whether the United States Congress will respond to such a call from the people and the President, if it comes.

Having participated in the work of Congress for the last ten years, I doubt it. The legislative measures needed to sustain the concept of community are vital ones—a broadened Trade Expansion Act, Congressional adherence to an enlarged International Monetary Fund, a sustained aid program, a bold legislative attack on unemployment, adherence to an invigorated OECD. Congress as it is now constituted, faced with such a legislative program, could well prove insufficiently responsive and responsible.

Congress last took a thorough reforming look at itself in the Legislative Reorganization Act of 1946. The act stemmed

from the work of the Joint Committee on the Organization
of Congress, with the late Sen. Robert M. La Follette, Jr., of
Wisconsin as chairman and with Rep. (now Senator) Mike
Monroney of Oklahoma as vice-chairman. The Act increased
Congressional salaries and staff, required the registration of
lobbyists, reduced the number of standing committees, and
relieved the workload by banning certain types of private bills.

But it is now clear that the Legislative Reorganization Act
of 1946 failed to touch the main causes which make Congress
less than responsive to the national will. The Act simply did
not deal with the malapportionment of Congressional seats,
or with the increasing power of an entrenched minority to
block the will of the majority—whether by a Senate filibuster,
the House Rules Committee, a dictatorial committee chairman, or an unresponsive committee.

Yet the duties and responsibilities of Senators and Representatives have increased enormously since 1946. Two other
events of that same year dramatically emphasize this. One was
the Employment Act of 1946, in which the Federal government accepted its responsibility for maximum employment and
production. This has moved Congress into economics in a way
no one dreamed of.

The second climacteric of 1946 was the beginning of the
Cold War. This, too, thrust Congress into the age of nuclear
weapons, of vast continuing armaments, of space, of new con-
stellations of nations concerned with new problems.

Always before, America had time, sometimes generations,
in which to attempt solutions for its problems. But now, as
Prof. James MacGregor Burns points out, "there is grave
doubt that history still allows us this cushion."

The problem is not that the national legislature has lost
power. Compared to the parliaments of France, Pakistan, and
most of Latin America, not to mention Africa and Asia, Congress has if anything asserted its relative power vis-à-vis the
executive.

Nor has Congress shown lack of ability to initiate. The labor legislation of 1959 was largely the work of Sen. John F. Kennedy and others in Congress. The Peace Corps originated as a child of Congress. Initiatives in Congress, much more than in the Administration, were responsible for the Trade Expansion Act of 1962.

Congress can surely become, as former Rep. Jerry Voorhis of California once said:

. . . not merely an agency that says yes or no to Executive proposals, but an agency capable of, and actually performing, the function of bringing forth its own constructive program for the needs of the people of this Nation. Thus, it will take its place and keep its place as an altogether coequal branch of our Government.*

But first Congress must put into effect those reforms which now prevent its exercising independent greatness. It must eliminate the evils of malapportionment and gerrymandering and assure an equal, free exercise of the right to vote in Federal elections. It must eliminate roadblocks to action, such as the power of filibuster in the Senate and abuses of the Rules Committee's power in the House. It must make leadership more effective and less diffuse by gaining control over the committee system. And it must lessen the workload of its members on less consequential matters in order to free them for the needed study and debate of major policy.

Let us look in turn at each of these four failures that make Congress unequal to its task.

An unrepresentative Congress. Although American voters are in theory equal in their right to elect their Federal Representatives, in fact they suffer from serious inequalities.

Malapportionment of Congressional districts is one of the major sources of this inequality. In 21 of the 42 states that have more than one Congressional district, the largest district

* *Congressional Record,* Jan. 18, 1945, p. 363.

has at least twice as many people as the smallest district. This gives voters in the small districts twice the weight in Congress of voters in large districts. Many rural districts are greatly overrepresented; some urban, and many suburban, districts are greatly underrepresented. Under such conditions, if the House reflects the sentiment of the voters of the country, it is pure accident. Although it may be uncertain who gains over-all from this distortion of our system, it is certain that representative government suffers.

Fortunately, the Supreme Court has apparently opened a way to correct Congressional malapportionment through its 1962 decision in *Baker v. Carr*. That decision, in invalidating a palpably unfair apportionment of seats in the Tennessee legislature, suggests that an unequal distribution of seats in the Congress would be likewise invalidated. Nevertheless, Congress should act to include in the permanent apportionment act the requirement unwisely dropped in 1929 that Congressional districts be "contiguous and compact territory containing as nearly as practicable an equal number of inhabitants."

The representative character of Congress is also sadly impaired by restrictions on the exercise of the franchise and the senseless variety in voting regulations for Federal office. The most glaring problems of this type occur in the Deep South, where literacy tests, poll taxes, and similar devices have been used effectively to keep Negroes from registering and to hold down the vote to "manageable proportions."

Progress is being made in this area also. Passage of the Constitutional amendment outlawing the poll tax as a prerequisite for voting in Federal elections and provisions in the civil rights act for the registration of Negroes despite the obduracy of registrars promise to wipe out the worst abuses. But other potential voters are being needlessly and haphazardly disenfranchised by long residence qualifications and inconvenient, complex registration procedures. For example, some states require at least two years' residence before enfranchisement. These impediments should be eliminated to allow broad, equal participation in Federal elections.

But even if Congressmen were elected from equal, fair districts under equal, fair voting laws, Congress would still not be able to fulfill its role unless it eliminated the serious roadblocks that now prevent it from acting effectively.

Roadblocks to action. Ours is a government of balanced powers. The power of the majority in Congress is balanced, under the Constitution, by the existence of two Houses; by the powers of the 50 states; by the veto of the President; by the independence of the Federal judiciary. But in less than a quarter-century Congressional government by majority rule has received two additional checks, not provided for in our Constitutional system. These two checks—the filibuster in the Senate and the Rules Committee in the House—effectively prevent the two branches of the legislature from acting at all on many of the great issues of the times.

The procedural device of the Senate to obstruct the will of the majority is Rule 22, which provides that cloture, an agreement to limit debate so that a measure may be voted on, may be invoked only by a vote of two-thirds of the Members of the Senate present and voting. Unless this extraordinary two-thirds majority can be mustered, therefore, it is possible for a minority of the Senate—thirty Senators or so— to prevent a measure's ever coming up for a vote. The number of Senators required to bear the actual brunt of the filibuster is even less. The Southern leadership in the Senate has evolved the "two-platoon" system. Under this, if some 18 Senators are determined to filibuster, they can divide themselves into two platoons of nine each; groups of three can then hold the floor for eight-hour periods, talk around the clock, and then take a day off before returning to the floor. Unless broken by cloture, a filibuster can go on until the session ends or until the proponents of the measure tire and give up.

There have been repeated attempts over the last ten years to change Rule 22 so that cloture can be voted with something less than a two-thirds majority. At the start of the session in 1963, the Senate spent more than three weeks debating the proposal of Senator Clinton P. Anderson of New Mexico to amend Rule 22 so that a mere three-fifths of the Senators present and voting could invoke cloture. This would still give the minority easy opportunity for extended debate. Anderson and his colleagues took the position that a change in the Senate Rules was not itself subject to Rule 22, and that a mere majority could vote to close debate and bring the proposed rule change up for a vote.

Their position was not sustained. The attempt to amend Rule 22 finally failed when a cloture motion made to bring this to a vote, while it got a majority, failed to get a two-thirds majority. The vote of 54 in favor of cloture and a rules change, and 42 against, fell ten votes short of the two-thirds majority needed. But this was the first time that the proponents of a rules change succeeded in getting a majority. And they did so although President Kennedy took no part in the controversy.

On the House side, the Rules Committee has been a roadblock to the consideration of legislation for a quarter of a century. In the House, important legislation approved by a committee must be considered by the full House under a resolution or "rule" granted by the Committee on Rules. This procedure was originally intended only as a means of setting out how long a bill was to be debated and what amendments would be in order. The Rules Committee was to be a sort of "traffic cop" regulating the traffic from the 19 standing committees to the House. But when FDR's majority in the House declined in the midterm election of 1938, Democratic and Republican conservatives on the Rules Committee joined forces to deny the House an opportunity to consider legislation that the committee opposed. Ten years later, after the liberal victory in the 1948 elections, the House at the start of the 1949 session adopted the so-called "21-day rule." Under that rule, if the Rules Committee failed to report within 21 days any resolution for consideration by the House of any public bill favorably reported by a committee of the House, the Chairman of the committee reporting the bill could call up the resolution, and the Speaker was required to recognize him.

The rule worked very well for the 81st Congress in 1949 and 1950. During the first session, it brought an anti-poll-tax bill and a rivers-and-harbors bill to the House floor for a successful vote, and it forced action on housing and minimum wage bills. During the second session, it enabled the House to vote for the National Science Foundation, Alaska and Hawaii statehood legislation, the National Minerals Act, a veterans'-hospital bill, and a joint resolution for United States participation in certain international organizations. By resort to the 21-day rule, eight measures were brought to the floor, and seven of them passed. Moreover, the fact that it was available forced the Rules Committee to act on other measures which would have been bottled up but for its existence.

But the reform was short-lived. The liberals lost seats again in the 1950 election, and the 82nd Congress, which took office in 1951, promptly repealed the 21-day rule. The Rules Committee has continued to be a roadblock to legislation ever since.

A number of important pieces of legislation, including school construction and the omnibus housing bill, were blocked from reaching the floor by the Rules Committee in the closing days of the 86th Congress in the summer of 1960.

At the start of the first Kennedy Congress in January, 1961, the Kennedy forces settled on the strategy of upping the membership of the Rules Committee from 12 members to 15. Under the 12-member committee, Rep. Howard Smith of Virginia and Rep. William Colmer of Mississippi, both conservative Democrats, usually sided with the Republican minority of four, leaving a 6-6 deadlock. Enlarging the membership to 15—ten Democrats and five Republicans—was seized upon as a means of breaking the deadlock and permitting legislation to reach the floor.

Chairman Smith of the Rules Committee, confronted by the move to enlarge the membership from 12 to 15, agreed "to interpose no obstacles in the Rules Committee to the five major bills that the President has publicly announced as his program for this session" if the House would only leave the Committee on Rules membership at the existing 12. The House refused the offer, and on Jan. 31, 1961, by a vote of 217 to 212, increased the membership to 15 for the duration of the 87th Congress.

The House's reason for doing so is summed up by the statement made during the debate on Jan. 31, 1961, by Speaker Rayburn:

The House of Representatives is elected every 2 years, and after the legislative committees hold hearings, after executive session, when every *i* is dotted and every *t* is crossed, and when the chairman comes to the Committee on Rules—and I do not say Rules Committee, because that is not the proper designation; it is the Committee on Rules—comes to the leadership of the House and wants a rule after all of that consideration, I think that the Committee on Rules should grant that rule whether its membership is for the bill or not. I think this House should be allowed on great measures to work its will, and it cannot work its will if the Committee on Rules is so constituted as not to allow the House to pass those things.*

Enlarging the Rules Committee to 15 in the 1961–62 Congress resulted in more bills reaching the floor. But even the 15-man Committee still acted as a partial roadblock. It bottled up to the end, and prevented a vote on the President's mass transportation bill, his youth conservation corps bill, and his

* *Congressional Record,* Jan. 31, 1961, p. 1508.

bill to provide grants for medical and dental school construction. In all, the Rules Committee during the 87th Congress refused to grant rules to 34 significant measures, either by voting down a rule or by taking no action. On other measures, the Rules Committee delayed as long as nine months before reporting a rule. In still other cases, the Rules Committee forced changes in various bills as a condition of granting a rule.

The 15-man Rules Committee expired with the 87th Congress. Another fight took place at the opening of the 88th Congress on Jan. 9, 1963, when the House voted to make the 15-man committee permanent, by a vote of 235–196.

But the delaying and blocking tactics of the Rules Committee have continued in the 88th Congress, though on a lesser scale. A remedy for the roadblocking proclivities of the Rules Committee lies in the 21-day rule which was in effect in 1949 and 1950.

The House Committee on Rules possesses another power which can be used to prevent the House from exercising its will. This is the power to prevent a House-Senate conference on important bills—those raising or spending money—which have been approved by both House and Senate but in different forms.

The 1960 session of Congress provides a good illustration of this. A bill (H.R. 10128) to provide financial assistance to states for school construction passed the House, 206 to 198, on May 6, 1960. On June 8, the Senate amended the House bill by substituting its own version. The Senate requested a conference with the House. The chairman of the House Committee on Education and Labor, which was responsible for the bill, requested unanimous consent to take the bill from the Speaker's table, disagree with the Senate's amendments, and set up a conference. Upon one member's objection, the bill was automatically referred to the House Committee on

Rules. Here it languished and died when the Committee on Rules refused a special order by a 7-to-5 vote.

This power of the Committee on Rules to block a conference is an extremely broad one. Most major legislation requires a conference. Thus the House Committee on Rules is given a second opportunity to frustrate action on important bills.

A remedy that has been suggested to prevent the Rules Committee from stopping a bill's being sent to conference is the enactment of the so-called 7-day rule. Under this proposed amendment to the rules, if the Rules Committee fails to send a bill passed by both Senate and House to conference within seven days, the chairman of the House legislative committee which reported the bill in the first place is permitted to call it up for consideration, and have it sent to conference by a majority vote of the House.

Opponents of Rules Committee reform frequently claim that a majority of the House can work its will despite the Rules Committee, and hence that a reform is unnecessary. But the three existing procedures—the discharge petition, suspension of the rules, and Calendar Wednesday—which are claimed to have this magic power, are in fact grossly inadequate.

The discharge petition is an extremely difficult and time-consuming procedure. A majority, now 218, of the 435 House members must sign a petition discharging from committee a House bill or resolution. A majority of 218, of course, is a considerably larger majority than is required to pass a bill on the floor, where a number of members can always be relied upon to be absent. Moreover, a large number of members habitually refuse to sign discharge petitions even though they may be for the bill in question. Most important of all, the public has no way of knowing who has signed or not signed a discharge petition, since the petition is kept private at the

Clerk's Desk, and is not published in the *Congressional Record*. Hence, the procedure flouts an important principle of democratic government—that the representatives of the people stand up and be counted.

Another procedure which bypasses the Rules Committee is suspension of the rules. If the Speaker wishes to recognize a member for such a purpose, he may do so on the first or third Monday of each month. But it requires a two-thirds vote for passage rather than a simple majority. And only 40 minutes of debate—wholly inadequate—is allowed.

A third device for bypassing the Rules Committee is the so-called Calendar Wednesday procedure. Every Wednesday the Speaker can call the roll of the legislative committees in alphabetical order, and the chairman of each committee is empowered to call up for consideration and vote any one bill which has previously been voted on by his committee. The hitch to Calendar Wednesday is that action must be finished in the same legislative day. The procedure is thus vulnerable to dilatory tactics of every type by opponents of the bill.

A recent attempt to use the Calendar Wednesday procedure illustrates how meaningless it is. A youth training bill was reported favorably by the House Education and Labor Committee on Aug. 2, 1961. As of Sept. 19, 1962, more than a year later, the House Committee on Rules had taken no action on the proposal. Representative Carl Perkins of Kentucky, sponsor of the youth training bill, attempted to use the Calendar Wednesday procedure. As it happened, the alphabetical call of the committees that day would have begun with Foreign Affairs, and nineteen other committees would have had to be called before the Education and Labor Committee would have been reached, thus giving Perkins his chance. The House never got that far, however, because members opposed to the bill consumed almost three hours with procedural roll calls and demands that the House Clerk read the journal of the previous day in full. Perkins, realizing that his supporters would be dwindling away as the evening wore on, gave up the fight.

Diffusion of leadership.   Woodrow Wilson, in his 1885 book, *Congressional Government,* said:

The leaders of the House are the Chairmen of the Standing Committees. Indeed, to be entirely accurate, the House has as many leaders as there are leading classes of legislation—each committee goes its own way at its own pace.

This is still largely true today. To the extent that Congress consists of government by committee, it diffuses the role of leadership in both the Presidency and the Congress.

The crux of the committee system is the seniority system. Once on a committee, a member of House or Senate who gets re-elected rises inexorably to the chairmanship, if he lives that long. Senators and Congressmen with the greatest seniority tend to be from safe constituencies. These are usually rural constituencies from the Democratic South or Republican Midwest. This gives committee chairmen a built-in conservative leaning.

The powers of a committee chairman are important. By neglecting to call meetings, he can prevent action. He also may control the agenda of committee action: by refusing to put a bill on the agenda, he can block action. The chairman also appoints subcommittees, manages bills on the floor, and heads the conference committee when differences with the other chamber need to be worked out.

The rules of both Senate and House with respect to committee procedures sketch out a few general principles, and let it go at that. While some committees, such as the House Committee on Interior and Insular Affairs, have model sets of rules, almost half of the Congressional committees still have rules which permit domination by the committee chairman.

What is the remedy? Frequently it is suggested that the

seniority rule be abrogated, and that chairmen be elected by their committee. I question whether the alternative of election would really be an improvement. The electioneering involved in becoming chairman might well create so many obligations that the committee would be mortgaged for years to come after every election.

In any event, Congress is most unlikely to change the seniority rule. For one thing, while first-term Congressmen are traditionally opposed to seniority, it is surprising how quickly they decide that the system has virtues they never perceived. Since the majority of Congress is reasonably senior, seniority is not likely to go.

But the sting can be removed from seniority if the rules of committees are so reformed that the committee chairman is the servant rather than the master of the majority of the committee. If each House had minimum rules of performance for its individual committees, the chairman could still be a genial and respected gavel-wielder, but could not be a despot. Such a minimum set of rules would permit a majority of members to convene meetings, consider legislation, vote on it, designate the member to preside when the chairman is absent, establish ground rules for subcommittees, and make up the agenda.

There remains the problem of the committee that refuses to report to the floor a measure that Congress as a whole ought to pass upon. Committees are intended to give the Congress the benefit of their judgment, but not to substitute their judgment for that of the whole Congress. The problem, then—and a difficult one—is to preserve the real values of the committee system while eliminating its flagrant abuses.

The best solution on the House side, I believe, is to reduce from 218 to 150 the number of signatures required on a discharge petition to bring a bill out of an intractable committee and to the floor.

The present 218 signatures, for reasons previously stated, are practically impossible to attain. Since the House in 1910 first adopted the discharge rule, only two bills have been enacted into law through the discharge method: the Fair Labor Standards Act of 1938, and the Federal Pay Raise Act of 1960.

Reducing the magic number to a reasonable 150 (out of a possible 435) would simply restore the number in effect during the eleven-year period between 1924 and 1935. This should ensure that a bill labeled "urgent" by the President could at least have a fair chance of coming before the entire House. As one who has worked on a number of discharge petitions, I can testify that the first 150 signatures come easy.

Moreover, the mere existence of a 150-signature discharge petition would tend to induce legislative committees to report out, rather than bury, bills that have widespread support.

It is sometimes argued that the present 218-signature rule "protects" members from having to vote on a flood of ill-considered, demagogic measures that would ensue were the number reduced. The case for "protecting" a House member from having to stand up and record his vote seems to me less compelling than the case for protecting the public's right to have major issues publicly acted on by the legislature.

In any case, the discharge petition is not likely to become a common means of bringing legislation to the floor. From 1910 (when the discharge rule was adopted) through 1962, only 810 discharge petitions have been filed, of which only 20 succeeded. But of these 20 bills thus brought to the floor, 16 have then passed the House. Significantly, the average number of discharge petitions filed annually during the 1924–35 period, in which only 150 signatures were required, was lower (13) than the average number filed in all Congresses (30) since the rule was adopted. This suggests that during the period of easier discharge, committees were more reasonable in reporting out legislation.

Because the Senate lacks the House's discharge-petition

procedure, a different solution is needed. One possibility is to amend the Senate rules to provide that any bill recommended by the President may be called up for action on the floor of the Senate if the committee to which the bill has been assigned has after 60 days failed to report it out.

A "reform" sometimes suggested for preventing diffusion of leadership is to increase the term of Representatives from two years to four. This has been proposed both by believers in a strong Presidency, such as Prof. James MacGregor Burns, and by believers in a passive Presidency, such as former President Eisenhower. Making the Representative's term co-terminous with the Presidency would tend, undoubtedly, to give him more of a Presidential flavor. And the relief from running every two years would undoubtedly appeal to many.

In my view, House terms should be left as they are. Running for election every two years may be a considerable chore, but I can think of no better way of insuring the two-way educational process between Congressman and constituent which is the essence of the democratic process.

Workload of members. Members of the national legislature are increasingly conscious of the time they and their staffs must spend on performing needed services for constituents. Staffs have been increased in recent years, but every colleague I talk to tells me that the burden of administrative work has increased even more. As long ago as 1940, Rep. Luther Patrick described a Congressman's duties:

A Congressman has become an expanded messenger boy, an employment agency, getter-out of the Navy, Army, Marines, ward heeler, wound healer, troubleshooter, law explainer, bill finder, issue translator, resolution interpreter, controversy oil pourer, glad hand extender, business promoter, convention goer, civic ills skirmisher, veterans' affairs adjuster, ex-serviceman's champion, watchdog of the underdog.

The 1945 Joint Committee on the Organization of Congress which produced the La Follette–Monroney reform had this to say about Congressional distractions:

A high percentage of congressional time is devoted to matters of purely local or petty importance. . . .

Your committee believes that Congress should jealously guard its time for ample debate and consideration of matters of national and international importance. It seems hardly consistent to hear the excuse that congressional calendars are too crowded to take up and discuss issues of great national interest when so much time is devoted to these minor matters. Congress still tenaciously clings to many insignificant details which could be far better handled by the executive departments and the courts.*

Former Rep. Burr P. Harrison of Virginia said in a 1962 newspaper interview:

The various activities of Congress are in progress at the same time, like a three-ring circus. If one duty is to be done properly, it is likely another must be content with a lick and a promise.

Committees sit as the floor debate proceeds and constituents wait in the office. A Member busy in committee will be summoned by the bells to vote on the floor on a measure as to the merits of which he knows little, if anything, and as to the controversial aspects of which he has heard no debate.

A Member occupied on the floor or in his office will hurry to committee to propound a series of questions to a witness on points which the witness has discussed fully prior to his arrival. . . . In general, no one knows this week what Congress is going to do next week. . . . [This] is an intolerably vexatious, inefficient management of the time of its Members.

The assistant majority leader of the Senate, Sen. Hubert H. Humphrey, in an Apr. 7, 1963, *New York Times Magazine* article, pointed out that "many Members of the Senate and the House spend up to 90 per cent of their time—and the time of their staffs—answering mail, meeting with constituents and

* House Report 1675, 79th Congress, 2nd Session, pp. 24–25.

handling individual constituent complaints or requests." He went on to say:

In 1949 I moved into an office of four rooms. My staff and I had the use of two telephone lines. An average of 50 letters a day were received. Thirty telephone calls a day were considered heavy. A personal visit to the office by a constituent on any day was a special event. In 1962, my office had doubled to eight rooms. Now, 12 telephone lines funnel an average of 500 calls into the office each day, and I keep two private lines just to be sure I will be able to get through the crowded switchboard to reach my staff. One hundred and twenty personal visitors—not counting large groups of students and tourists—come into the office each day, about half of them constituents from my home State.

While the administrative burden on Congress has been thus increased, the challenge of the member's primary task—that of legislating—has likewise become greater. A member today must be informed about details of the national economy and of international affairs which were undreamed of a few years ago.

Two reforms—which have other important reasons for their adoption—would undoubtedly help relieve the average Congressman's workload.

One would be to set up an office of Administrative Counsel to perform for Congressmen much of the casework traditional in Congressional-constituent relations—social security cases, Veterans Administration matters, treatment and discharges in the military services, claims of discrimination in government contracts, civil service appointments and advancement, and so on. These now occupy an appalling amount of the time of a Congressman and his staff.

A Congressman handed a complaint by his constituent could refer the matter to the Administrative Counsel, who would then look into the controversy, either on the basis of the material submitted or on the basis of a full investigation.

Then the counsel would report his recommendations back to the Congressman concerned. Frequently, if the counsel's recommendation were in favor of the constituent, the erring administrative agency would have rectified the matter in the course of the investigation. If it had not, the member would undoubtedly wish to transmit the counsel's recommendations to the relevant agency with his own request for remedial action.

Such an Administrative Counsel would be an adaptation to American conditions of the generally similar office of Ombudsman, which has proved highly successful in Sweden since 1809 and in Finland since 1919. Similar offices were created in Japan in 1948, in Denmark in 1955, and in Norway and New Zealand in 1962. The Ombudsman, a sort of Robin Goodfellow who mediates between the citizen and the bureaucracy, has become a successful adjunct of democratic government.

After studying how the Ombudsman worked in other countries, I introduced legislation in July, 1963 (H.R. 7593) to set up a similar Administrative Counsel here.

In addition to freeing Congressmen for more important decision-making legislative duties, the Administrative Counsel would assist the private citizen in his relations with his government far better than a Congressional office, with its limited staff, could do. By the same token, it should act to prevent the endless increases in members' staffs. These have grown steadily in recent years. Today a Representative can have as many as 10 staff members in his Washington office, a Senator as many as 30. Senatorial office space has recently been increased, and on the House side members will soon have three, rather than two, offices. All of this presents endless new costs to the taxpayer, of course. Setting up the office of the Admininstrative Counsel could permit the leveling off of staff increments.

Second only to acting as a pleader and broker for constituents in the Congressional overload is the time and attention

Congress gives to the affairs of the District of Columbia. Since the 1870's, the Congress, and particularly the House and Senate District of Columbia Committees, have been the Board of Aldermen and the Mayor of the District, a city of three-quarters of a million.

Thus the program for the United States House of Representatives for July 22, 1963, consisted of the following:

DISTRICT DAY—5 BILLS

1. H.R. 6128   Record of stockholders of life insurance companies
2. H.R. 6350   Dental hygienists licensing examinations
3. H.R. 6353   Unemployment compensation information for D.C. Department of Public Welfare
4.   S.   489   Amending of small claims procedures before D.C. Court of General Sessions
5.   S.   490   Eliminating duplicate D.C. motor vehicle lien file

And the House of Representatives devoted its legislative day—as it does dozens of other legislative days during the year—to the primarily local business of the District of Columbia. All 535 Members of the Senate and the House are thus engaged in District of Columbia affairs. And the load on the two District committees amounts to many thousands of man-hours a year.

Limited home rule for the District of Columbia—one which would give the people of the District the right to elect their Board of Aldermen and other local officials, and govern their own local matters—subject always to Congressional veto— has been before the Congress since 1948.

The La Follette–Monroney Committee recommended home rule for the District of Columbia as a means of reducing the Congressional workload back in 1946:

The nation cannot afford the luxury of having its national legislative body and the District Committees in both the House and

Senate perform the duties of a city council for the District of Columbia.

In order to relieve the Congress of this extraneous work-load and enable it to develop full attention to national legislation we recommend that a plan for self-rule for the District of Columbia be provided as early as possible.

District home rule, of course, is not merely a device for enabling Congress to lighten its workload. Much more importantly, it would vindicate the American principle of suffrage and self-government. It would lay to rest the suspicion that self-government is being denied because a majority of the District's inhabitants are Negroes. If the residents of the District of Columbia are to be expected to work out their local problems as diverse as taxes and juvenile delinquency and schools and race relations and city planning and crime, they must be given the right and the duty of governing themselves. *

After 16 years of effort by home rule advocates, the House of Representatives has still never been allowed to vote on whether the District of Columbia should have home rule. The will of every President during this period, and the mandate of both political party platforms, has been set at naught.†

A remedy has been suggested for the impasse whereby the

* During the first 70 years of the 19th century, the District of Columbia did govern itself. But then Congress withdrew the right, and installed instead the present system, whereby Congress itself makes all the laws for the District and thus its citizens have nothing to say about it. They elect no aldermen, they elect no mayor, they elect no school board.

† Presidents Truman, Eisenhower, and Kennedy have all vigorously advocated local self-government for the District of Columbia. Home rule has been pledged by the political platforms of both major political parties in 1948, in 1952, in 1956, and in 1960.

Five times since 1948 the Senate has passed home rule legislation. The House, on the other hand, has never had the opportunity to vote on home rule. Since 1948, the District Committee has allowed no home rule bill to reach the floor of the House.

Hearings on home rule bills were held by the House District Committee in June and July, 1949, but were tabled by the committee on August 19. In October, 1949, then Rep. John F. Kennedy filed a petition in the House

House District Committee, hopelessly loaded for many years to come with opponents of home rule, could be prevented from further denying members of the House the right to vote on it. That device would be a change in the Rules of the House allowing any individual member of the District Committee to call up a home rule bill for floor action despite committee failure to report on it. Under this new rule, the home rule bill would be the business of the House until it was voted on, up or down. Most observers are convinced that a home rule bill would pass if it could be brought to a vote in the House.

Besides an Administrative Counsel and District home rule, there are other minor ways of relieving the Congressional workload.

Putting postmasters under the merit system, instead of keep-

---

to discharge the home rule bill passed by the Senate. Only 196 signatures were obtained instead of the 218 required.

In January, 1952, the Senate again passed a home rule bill. The House District Committee held hearings on home rule in March and April, 1952, but tabled the bill on May 9, 1952.

Home rule legislation was referred to the House District Committee in the 83rd Congress—1953-55—but no hearings were had.

The Senate on June 29, 1955, again passed a home rule bill, this time by a vote of 59 to 15. It was referred to the House District Committee, where no further action was taken.

On Apr. 30, 1958, the Senate again passed a home rule bill, this time by a vote of 61 to 22. The bill was sent to the House and referred to the District Committee, where no further action was taken.

On July 15, 1959, the Senate again passed a home rule bill. It was sent to the House, where it was referred to the District Committee. For the first time in years, the District Committee held hearings on home rule bills, lasting seven days in July, August, and September, 1959. No bill was reported out.

Discharge petitions for a home rule bill were filed in the House in July, 1959. By July, 1960, when Congress recessed for the national political conventions, 204 members—150 Democrats and 54 Republicans—had signed the petition, just short of the 219 signatures required.

In 1962, another discharge petition was filed, but again failed to get the required number of signatures.

ing them as political appointees, could save much time of
Senators who now spend many hours trying to pick the appli-
cant whose appointment will achieve the most political good
and the least political harm. As one Senator said, "Every time
I make an appointment, I make eleven enemies and one in-
grate."

Holding more joint meetings of Congressional committees
and subcommittees could likewise end much duplication of
time and effort. In July, 1963, tripartite sessions on the balance of payments were held by the Joint Economic Committee, the International Finance Subcommittee of the Senate
Committee on Banking and Currency, and its House counterpart. There should be more of this.

Applications of young men to the Service Academies, such
as West Point, Annapolis, and the Air Force Academy, could
well be handled by civil service examinations, rather than
by the time-consuming selection by a Senator or Representative. Many Congressmen now utilize the civil service method,
and have bowed out themselves.

Here, then, are the sick tissues of an ailing Congress—unrepresentative districts, built-in roadblocks to action, a Bal-
kanized committee system, and an errand-boy's workload that
diverts legislators from their primary duties.

Some of the surgery needed is already underway. Eliminating the gerrymandered district is in sight as a result of
Supreme Court decision, and the end of the poll tax via a constitutional amendment. Congress itself can be expected to improve its own housekeeping practices, ranging from closer
control over Congressional travel to full disclosure of situa-
tions causing conflicts of interest.

But the central ailment of the Congress—the power of a
minority to frustrate the will of the majority—is not so easily
solved, *for the simple reason that the obstructive minority is
not likely to preside at the liquidation of its own arbitrary*

power. As Goethe used to say of the German people, "They can never have a revolution, because the police will not permit it." The majority in Congress, however bent on reform, cannot have *its* revolution because the minority—one-third of a filibustered Senate, the House Rules or District of Columbia Committees, or a tyrannical committee chairman—will not permit it.

Reform of the Senate cloture rule has not been achieved, though a clear majority favor it, because a minority can filibuster against a change until a two-thirds vote is obtained to end the provision requiring a two-thirds vote. Reform of the Rules of the House has not been achieved, because proposals for reform—whether in specific detail or merely to appoint a commission to study and recommend reforms—go to the House Rules Committee, which refuses to do anything about them.

So the reformers' revolution languishes.

There are ways, though, if the public becomes concerned enough and vocal enough. The Presidential election of 1964 has not been decided in advance; both parties are under the impression that they can win, and will wish their parties' platforms to reflect publicly felt needs.

Suppose, then, that both Republican and Democratic 1964 platforms contained planks pledging a reform of the filibuster in the Senate (as they have before, it must be admitted); a 21-day rule for the House Rules Committee and a 7-day rule on conference reports; a 150-signature House discharge petition; and a change in the House rules so as to permit consideration of home rule for the District of Columbia.

A President pledged to support the change in the Senate cloture rule, who vigorously redeems his pledge when the Senate convenes in 1965, might just make the difference in picking up the ten votes needed to achieve that reform.

Prospects in the House could be even brighter, because there reform is achievable by a simple, rather than a two-thirds, majority vote. The House has just one day every two years when it can consider changes in its rules without asking leave of the House Rules Committee—the opening day of a new Congress, the next one due in January, 1965.

Assuming that the platform of the party in control so provided, the Speaker would be duty bound on that opening day to recognize a member to propose that the rules of the new House include an appropriate package of amendments, such as the 21-day rule, the 7-day rule, the 150-signature discharge petition, and District of Columbia home rule. The House could then proceed immediately to debate the proposals for change in the rules and get a record vote on them.

If the entire package failed to get a majority vote, the member recognized by the Speaker to present the changes could pursue the matter further, by deleting for successive votes the most controversial items in the package. Thus if the whole package failed to get a majority, there could be a record vote on each element in the package.

If the people want reform of Congress, it can be done. For Congress, as *Time* correspondent Neil MacNeil has said in his history of the House, *The Forge of Democracy*, reflects:

. . . the whole people, their weaknesses as well as their strengths, their foolishness as well as their wisdom, their prejudices as well as their tolerances, their fears as well as their courage.

The American people, if it catches the music needed to accompany a great American role in the free world community, can make Congress hear it too.

CHAPTER NINE

The Politics of Partnership

Whatsoever thy hand findeth to do,
Do it with thy might.

Ecclesiastes 10:10

The program here proposed for a free world community challenges the people of the United States and the other free world nations to their most creative action for human welfare and international order. In times of war and in response to the Soviet threat, we have dedicated ourselves and massed our resources. But our purposes were largely negative and defensive. In our efforts to build a better world order, our will has flagged and our deeds have proved too few or too weak.

Now a new, comprehensive agenda confronts the people of the free world. It envisages sustained, generation-long cooperation among all nations, developed and developing; an international organization that can be at once an instrument and a source of that cooperation; a vast increase in world trade and a new international monetary mechanism that will help bind nations together and harmonize their relationships; policies of aid and economic growth that will give to citizens of all nations an increasing measure of material benefits.

For the United States, this means the following action program:

1. We must grow faster and promptly bring our unemployment down to 3 per cent. The chief instruments of this policy should be a tax cut to boost demand larger than the

213

1963 proposal, reasonably low interest rates to avoid choking off economic expansion, and a work-and-learn program to provide immediate jobs and training to many thousands who would remain unemployed while the longer-term measures take effect.

2. In foreign policy, we must give high priority to unrelenting efforts to strengthen the Organization for Economic Cooperation and Development and through it to adopt the programs the free world needs in trade, payments, and aid.

3. In trade, we must work through the GATT for the widest and deepest possible free world tariff cuts, after amending our Trade Expansion Act to permit down-to-zero bargaining. If one or more principal countries refuse to cooperate, the others should still go ahead, and deny most-favored-nation treatment to the recalcitrant. The removal of nontariff obstacles to trade should proceed side by side with tariff reductions.

4. We must bring our international payments into balance promptly by cutting where it will do the least harm to our three big "deficit" items—military defense abroad, overseas capital investment, and untied foreign aid—while continuing to expand our receipts. At the same time, we should strive for an improved monetary mechanism to finance a country's deficit for at least a reasonable period, and to provide needed additions to the supply of international reserves.

5. In the field of aid, we must increase our assistance to the poor of the world and make our aid more effective by eliminating wild fluctuations in the size of the program, and uncertainties about its continuance. We should enlist broader public support and stimulate private aid efforts. We should also use trade as an instrument of aid by moving through the GATT to lower the barriers of the rich countries against goods from developing nations, including manufactured goods, while allowing the developing countries an interim period in which they can continue protection of their infant industries.

6. If Congress is to be responsive to such a program of

action, basic institutional reforms are needed. Congressional reform should be made an issue in the 1964 Presidential campaign, and in every political campaign thereafter until it is achieved.

It is a huge and demanding program. And since it is a program which, by definition, affects free peoples, there is left the question whether the American people are ready to understand, to respond to, and to stay with the concept of a free world community, and all it entails, for the generation which will surely be required to build it.

At the moment, it may seem that apathy, self-satisfaction and devotion to the *status quo* are the dominant characteristics of the people of many of the developed nations, particularly the United States. In America, it seems difficult indeed to interest the prosperous majority in the 6 per cent who are unemployed. The development of suburbia has helped to insulate these unconcerned citizens from any pangs of conscience. No longer do the wealthy live in the grand house on the hill, and overlook the daily misery of their fellow citizens. An old jingle recalls the former physical nearness of citizens in different economic circumstances:

> The golf course is so near the mill that almost every day,
> The little children hard at work can see the men at play.

But now the well-off are shielded by their freeways and acres of subdivisions, and the poor are invisible.

Even more remote are the poor of the developing nations whom Americans are asked to aid through their taxes. The average citizen is not moved to political passion by the problems of the GATT or the international monetary order. He remains suspicious of effective international organizations.

Yet throughout our history, the spirit of restless effort and the desire for creativity has continually triumphed over placidity and contentedness. The party of hope tends to win out over the party of memory.

But how is the energy needed to bring a free world community to reality to be released? For Americans, three ancient and venerated strains in American life that are also to be found in a free world community present powerful claims for support.

The first of these concepts is the idea of interdependence that was expressed so fully in the mutual helpfulness of our frontier life—the "barn-raising" where all the neighbors joined to build a barn.

If there is one lesson to be gleaned as we look out from the plateau of the mid-Sixties, it is that the people of the free world must all hang together or they will all hang separately. The poor nations cannot make the grade unless the rich ones will open their trade, regularize their aid, and rationalize the international monetary system. Without such an improved monetary mechanism, the United States—and other industrial countries—cannot attain full employment. Without expanded trade, the best preventive of inflation in the fully employed countries will be lost. Unless the United States keeps moving to make the Negro a first-class citizen, our moral authority will dwindle. Unless there is reform in the United States Congress so that the majority will can be expressed, responsible cooperative action with other nations will elude us.

These are some of the dimensions of the new interdependence.

The second strain is that of idealism, as reflected in the writings of Thomas Jefferson and in the great American documents—a belief that the right of social progress belongs, not to Americans alone, but to all mankind.

The Kennedy Administration's most successful single program, the Peace Corps, succeeded largely because the American people sensed in it the twin images of interdependence and idealism. The Peace Corps is interdependent because the developing nations need people to teach them, and we need the opportunity to learn about the rest of the world. The Peace Corps is idealistic because it gives its volunteers an opportunity to pursue, for a season, a completely unselfish goal.

The third strain is federalism, with its capacity to reconcile the need for common action in some spheres and the pursuit of independent and diverse courses of action in others. Although a free world community is not truly federal, to be sure, it would utilize elements of federalism that should appeal to Americans.

But more immediately, the development of support for the free world community is a political process. Indeed, it must become a political issue in the United States and in other free countries. President Johnson and other American leaders must take up the cause of the free world community and eloquently set forth its contribution to peace, freedom, welfare, and justice.

They will be serving not only in their role as leaders of the American people. They will also stimulate debate and discussion on the continent of Europe, where there have been too few voices raised in behalf of more aid, an improved monetary system, or a counterpart to the American Trade Expansion Act of 1962. There are elements in all of the major European political parties—the Christian Democrats, the Social Democrats, and the Liberals—ready to rally around the standard of a free world community if it is raised by effective leadership. Acceptance of the free world community by the people of democratic Europe will be reflected in the policies of their governments.

The time is ripe for the injection of this great new issue. Europe is in political ferment. In the United Kingdom, Germany, and Italy, changes of government are in prospect through the installation of new leadership in ruling parties or through victories of the present opposition. These changes promise to sweep away old commitments and rigidities of policy. In the Benelux and in most of the European Free Trade Association countries, slightly left-of-center governments seem in the cards.

But one enormous impediment to a free world community

is De Gaulle's France. Although De Gaulle's presidential term expires in 1965, it is probable that he or his nominee will be in line for election for another seven-year term. If so, the concept of a free world community will have to contend with De Gaulle and Gaullism for the critical years that lie ahead.

President de Gaulle's grand design can best be gleaned from his own memoirs, published in 1959:

I intended to assure France primacy in Western Europe by preventing the rise of a new Reich that might again threaten its safety; to co-operate with East and West and, if need be, contract the necessary alliances on one side or the other without ever accepting any kind of dependency; to persuade the states along the Rhine, the Alps, and the Pyrenees to form a political, economic, and strategic bloc and to press forward this organization as one of the three world powers and, should it become necessary, as the arbiter between the Soviet and the Anglo-American camps. Since 1940, my every word and act have been dedicated to establishing these possibilities.*

Let no one say that President de Gaulle's aims are not perfectly clear. He wants a minimum of American and British influence on the Continent. His vision of a united Europe does not extend much beyond the present Six in geography and an instrument of greater French power in policy. NATO may be useful for the moment, while France is developing her own nuclear weapons, but it should function largely without French participation. It will be time to talk of world disarmament when France is fully rearmed. Russia will one day recoil from China and seek new allies in Europe. The states of Middle Europe can be detached from Russian control and brought into a Europe under French leadership. Germany should remain split, to limit its power, retain its present outlook, and allow France to deal with the present Communist satellites of Middle Europe. Authoritarian government is preferable to

* Charles de Gaulle, *Memoirs,* Volume III, *Salvation* (N.Y., 1960), pp. 204–205.

parliamentary "inefficiency." And the UN is to be systematically down-graded!

This set of attitudes, while fairly appalling, need not spell total conflict between De Gaulle and the ideal of a free world community. A rejuvenated France could find all the glory that a Gaullist patriot could ask for as a major partner in such a vast new enterprise. But if worst comes to worst, the United States must resist the temptation to react to Gaullism with negative action of our own.

Our response to De Gaulle's moves toward autarchy cannot be a world-wide return to attempts to build self-sufficiency in every country at enormous economic and social costs. There are already tendencies in this neo-isolationist direction. We should instead pursue policies that will liberalize trade, increase interdependence, and promote economic efficiency despite contrary policies by France or countries associated with her.

De Gaulle's policy would undermine NATO. Yet in our response, we cannot concentrate all on an attempt to build up NATO. NATO must, of course, be maintained and even strengthened by the greater European participation in strategic planning and targeting that is already taking place. But mere negative anticommunism and fear of Soviet military action do not by themselves promise any lasting success.

De Gaulle's policy is based on the creation of a new exclusive power center—a third force—comprised of countries in a particular geographic area "along the Rhine, the Alps, and the Pyrenees." America should not champion a rival policy which, though different in its exclusions, is alike in its exclusiveness. Exclusiveness—be it based on geography, such as contiguity to the Atlantic Ocean, on history, or on race—cannot meet the needs of the compacted modern world. This exclusive basis is the defect of all Atlantic partnership schemes. The defect is compounded in the concept of an Atlantic partnership between a united Europe and the United States insofar as the European union that is to grow out of the present Six excludes even some free European states.

The concept of Atlantic partnership has another serious defect. It apparently requires for its realization the completion of European unity some years hence. In effect, we are to give the Six a patent, and announce that we shall be viewing the drawing together of the nations as purely a spectator sport until, a generation hence, they tell us that Europe is united, and now *we* can start. In the meantime, the immense benefits of freer trade, stable payments, increased interdependence and faster growth, which have been eagerly grasped in Europe, are to be largely withheld from the United States and the rest of the free world. For us to insist on so self-immobilizing a concept of partnership is to push ourselves into a bottle and draw the cork in after us.

Admittedly, present sacrifices would be justified if this purely Atlantic-partnership approach would lead in one great advance to the ultimate goal of free world community. But the concept of building ever-larger blocs on the theory that when power centers reach roughly equal size, they will merge, or be more disposed to cooperate is, to say the least, unproved. On the contrary, history suggests that the emergence of a new power bloc is likely to be accompanied by intense egotism and nationalism. The process both engenders and feeds upon new fears and rivalries.

In contrast to narrow power-bloc policies is the challenge of building a free world community. It is open, not exclusive. Its creation can start immediately, not wait for years. It is a positive effort to build anew, not a mere reaction to the world plan of others, Communist or Gaullist. And yet, paradoxically, it is a better means of defending ourselves against the dangers of inimical international developments than any of the negative policies to which we may be tempted.

Most important of all, it is feasible. It is something we can do now, and do with all our might.

Index

ABOUT THE AUTHOR

Congressman Henry S. Reuss of Wisconsin is presently serving his fifth term in the House of Representatives. He is Chairman of the Banking and Currency Committee's Subcommittee on International Finance and of the Joint Economic Committee's International Exchange and Payments Subcommittee. Congressman Reuss is a graduate of Cornell University and Harvard Law School.